NORFOLK AND
CHANCE

CONFESSIONS OF A QUIZ MASTER

Steve Roy

v

Thanks to everyone who has helped askTony in particular

Karen, Cristina, Gary, Derya, Dad, Liz, Natalie
Sonia, Anita, Darners, Bob the Cat, Darrell,
Roy Walker,
Tone, Jenny, Paul H, Mandy, Joanne, Kate, Marian,
Doug, Alan, Jamie, Heidi, Matthew, Craig, June.

And anyone who has booked, attended, or cancelled
an askTony quiz night over the last 20 years

CONTENTS

1 QUIZ TEAM AGUILERA

I have always liked TV quiz shows. As a child my favourite was probably Bullseye with the great Jim Bowen. Look at what you could have won. Particularly if the contestants lived in a tenth floor flat and the prize was some garden furniture or a speedboat. The darts expert Tony Green who called the scores when the celebrity darts player threw for charity always used to tell the dart thrower that the audience had given them a nice round of applause. Great memories and thanks to youTube and Challenge TV these shows will never be lost to future generations.

Ted Rogers and his dusty bin on 3-2-1 was a bit more of a mystery to me. There would be a little bit of quiz action at the beginning where the contestants could literally win tens of pounds. Then there would be forty minutes of pretty dull cabaret acts before some very random clues were left. Eventually an object led to either a big prize or a dustbin. Here is an example:

The Arches Might Provide a Clue
Not Strolling But He's Going To

The accompanying prop was some sheet music. The solution was so simple. Ted explained that the first three letters of arches gave you arc. You then needed to take the letters h e and s away as "he's going to". You were left with the word arc. You then needed to rearrange that with sheet music, which gave you Music Maestro Please. Which meant that you had won the British Leyland Maestro – a car.

Winner Takes It All with Jimmy Tarbuck combined questions with a bit of gambling although I never really understood the logic. One question, five possible answers all at different odds. But obviously one of the answers was right so unlike sport, the result is known before the question is asked. The answer to the question was obviously the one with the shortest odds. Maybe I was missing something.

Family Fortunes had various hosts but peaked when Les Dennis took over. I had the good fortune to meet Les at a Cricklewood Bingo Hall in 1996 after a lager-fuelled night out. Les had been booked to appear on stage once the bingo finished. It must have been coming up to 11 o'clock when the Liverpudlian comic took the microphone. He surprised the audience by belting out a few tunes then promptly took his leave. Looking back and reading his excellent autobiography, Must the Show Go On, 1996 was a low point for Les. He went on to establish himself as a Roy family favourite with a dazzlingly brilliant portrayal of a reformed burglar as the character Michael Rodwell in Coronation Street.

Catchphrase was another favourite with Irishman Roy Walker at the helm. A staple of Sunday night teatime television, it ran for thirteen years before the ITV bosses decided Roy's face did not fit and replaced him with a younger man. The show promptly collapsed in the ratings and disappeared from the screens for 15 years only to be revived in 2013.

Less of a quiz show and more of a game show was Treasure Hunt featuring firstly Anneka Rice and then less successfully Annabel Croft. There was great excitement when Anneka appeared at the bridge in our town centre one episode, although she spent the next forty-five minutes visiting places I had never heard of. The premise of the show where contestants solved clues by simply looking up reference books and getting the occasional clue from Wincey Willis probably wouldn't work in the internet age, but the show did also make a comeback this century with Dermot Murnaghan at the helm.

With these shows as inspiration, I think the first quiz night I ever staged was for a New Year's Eve party my parents were having when I was about fifteen. During that year I had been operating the sound system at the local church for the weekly Sunday service. Surprising you might think that the church had a sound system but it was a big place and although often there were no more than 30 people, when the vicar spoke from his pulpit a lot of the pensioners couldn't hear him so he needed amplification.

The church sound system was incredibly expensive and unnecessarily sophisticated. It had several lapel microphones with battery packs, one of which I would clip to the vicar and he would hide the pack in his robe.

The sound work was unpaid and in truth extremely boring as the Sunday service would regularly go on for almost two hours and as you had to constantly fade up or fade down the priest depending on what has happening, there wasn't much opportunity to read a paper or do anything more interesting.

Knowing I was going to be doing this New Year's quiz, and aware that the vicar had been invited to the party, I thought it would be a nice idea to include a little clip of the vicar singing in the guess the voice round. For this I had recorded several celebrity voices from the radio (1989 this was - so no internet). I had been able to keep the vicar's microphone on during a particularly tuneful rendition of I Saw Three Ships but had diverted the output to a tape rather than to the speaker.

When the celebrity voices round came on, there was a murmur of anguished surprise when the flat tones of the vicar came out of Dad's Amstrad stereo, and the cleric's beetroot face gave the game away. He didn't speak to me much after that, which wasn't a big disappointment to me as it turned out that like many other vicars he was revealed to be a bit of wrong 'un, but best not to go into that...

After leaving school in 1992 quiz nights did not feature at all in my three years at university in London. I got involved working for the student newspaper and in the final year began making a digital version of that as the web had just begun and people were starting to build homepages.

That experience led me to get a six-week placement at The Telegraph in Canary Wharf in the spring of 1995, and then a longer spell working in Oxford part of the Express Newspapers group. It was only when I returned to London in 1996 that a quiz night resurfaced.

I had joined a company called Redwood who were a magazine publisher specialising in creating customer magazines for household names like Boots and Marks & Spencer. I joined as part of a very small team looking to build websites for these brands, and we had some interesting meetings with Greenpeace, Help The Aged, and various other outfits, as well as an early meeting with Marks & Spencer whose main stipulation for their website was that the homepage must feature a big picture of their chairman. I have just checked their latest version and that requirement appears to have been dropped.

The real significance of Redwood though in terms of this book and my life was that the company had a quiz night. It took place at the Glasshouse Stores in Soho and was compered by a man called Richard who was a lovely fella fond of the finer parts of society, and as such there would be quite a lot of questions about croquet, classical music and the like.

Richard left the company shortly into my time at Redwood, and after about a six-month gap various people started asking when the next quiz night was going to be. I volunteered to host it and a date was arranged.

The first task was to find a new venue as The Glasshouse Stores had banned the company following an incident with a fire extinguisher at the end of the previous quiz. The Glasshouse was one of that rare breed of pubs who at the time exclusively stocked Sam Smith beer. Mr. Smith is a lovely drop but the problem you have is if guests drink more than 2 pints of the stuff, things get very messy. If venues do insist on stocking and serving high strength lager, quiz participants standing on tables and raucous behaviour is going to result. Luckily being based in central London there were a few alternative venues to choose from, although most of them were just pubs that lacked the space for a hundred people in a dedicated room. After a few lunchtimes searching I found a place called Los Locos just off Covent Garden, which had a strapline that nobody was ugly after 2am.

Locos was primarily a nightclub that only got busy after 10pm so was perfect for the quiz night as it was free to hire, and we got exclusive use until 10pm. It had a DJ booth in the centre with alcove seating all the way round.

It was there I learnt the basics of hosting a quiz night. I probably ran two or three in the late nineties, and they were reasonably successful. The best team at Redwood was made up of some company veterans called The Betty and Ray Savage Dancers, and in the build-up to each quiz, there would be a lot of banter as to whether the Dancers could be beaten. Often the best way was for a group from advertising and editorial to form a mega-team consisting of about twelve people.

I left Redwood in April 2000 and apart from coming back to host another quiz night for them in late 2001, the idea of running quiz nights as a business had not yet occurred to me as I was busy with other things. I started a new job with ITN and was also trying to get an internet business off the ground.

Inspired by a colleague at Redwood called Tony, an expert on everything, and the emergence of search engines in the late 1990s, I had set up a website called askTony where users could type in a question and, instead of search results getting displayed, the user would get a response from a human who had researched the answer.

The site proved quite successful and generated a fair bit of publicity. The most positive was a piece in the internet trade magazine New Media Age:

> A new British Web site is offering free personal-
> ised Web searching. The catch? It uses man not
> machine. Called Ask Tony, the site (www.ask-
> tony.com) uses a team of volunteers to deal with
> queries on any subject and, in its first week, it dealt
> with 500 questions, the toughest one being: 'What
> came first - the chicken or the egg?' (makes a nice
> change from 'why is the sky blue?' - Ed). Users send
> requests on the Web site and results are e-mailed
> back to them.

> Founder Steve Roy says: "About 20% of inquiries so
> far relate directly to where can I buy goods. Other
> popular subjects include music, business research,
> and trivia." So no porn then. The big question,
> though, has still to be answered: Who is Tony? Ap-
> parently, it is a secret

Unfortunately, it also proved to be the undoing as I didn't
have enough researchers to cope with the volume of questions users were asking, a fact that didn't go unnoticed by the
Daily Mail:

> The only website which failed to respond was
> askTony, a British site which employs internet re-
> searchers to find answers to your questions. The
> website has been so inundated with enquiries -
> more than 10,000 - that they are temporarily un-
> able to respond until the site has been relaunched.

The truth was that although several researchers had signed
up, there was only one who was any good and she lived in
New York. Credit to her, she would answer loads of questions
each day, for no money whatsoever.

The site was simple. Visitors would be presented with a

form, they would type in their question, and the question would then be fired off to the researchers. A researcher could mark it as answered, send off a reply, and that would then stop another researcher from picking it up.

When we got to about a thousand questions and answers the database became searchable as we were starting to receive questions that had already been answered.

I wrote this up as a business plan and took it to the directors at Redwood to see if they would be interested in developing the idea. It did not really fit their business model so not surprisingly they said no. I also took the idea to several venture capitalists who rightly pointed out there was no clear revenue path beyond advertising. So the original version of askTony did not go any further and the site quietly died a few months later.

The postscript to this episode is only a few months later premium rate text messaging launched, and this proved a perfect mechanism for bringing in the revenue the original concept needed. And lo it came to pass that several sites launched pretty much with the same format, except this time questions had to be submitted via text. These sites were then joined by expert sections in both yahoo and google.

With the original concept for askTony not viable, I started to investigate whether quiz nights would be something I could turn into a business. A few colleagues who had left Redwood had approached me to see if I wanted to run a quiz night for their new companies. The old askTony website was taken down and replaced with a brand new one advertising quiz nights.

At around the same time an old friend from university spent the same amount of money creating a new website offering tips on how to save money. Twelve years later Martin Lewis sold MoneySavingExpert.com for £78 million.

Photo 1 That first quiz at home featuring the vicar, possibly around 1991

2 NO EYE DEAR

In early 2002 I was in the process of changing jobs, and about to get married. Somewhere between my stag weekend in Cork in early March, and the wedding at the end of April, a big moment arrived for askTony quiz nights. We received our first ever commercial booking.

The company in question I will keep a secret, but you can find them in the FTSE 100 and they've got an office near Temple. From early conversations with the client it was clear this was going to be a big event. The quiz would be held in one of their large conference rooms, and all the catering and drinks would be provided by their in-house team. I could use their internal sound system and connect a laptop to their video wall, which at the time was state of the art.

The organiser claimed there would be at least two hundred people attending so in one of the arrangement calls I said I would bring along four assistants to help me do the scoring and marking. I remember writing some of the questions in April 2002 well in advance of the quiz itself which was mid-May.

I then forgot all about the quiz as I got married on 27th April 2002 and subsequently went on a lovely honeymoon (Jamaica? No she accompanied me voluntarily). Immediately on returning I started a new job outside London, and soon the big quiz day arrived. I arrived at the client's offices just after 5pm and was joined by one of my assistants shortly afterwards. It was clear we had underdressed as my newly arrived askTony t-shirts were not blending in with what was obviously a very suited corporate culture. The team names had been agreed in advance but there were various last-minute changes before the scoring spreadsheet could be loaded into the laptop. I tested the microphone, connected my laptop, and checked whether the audio rounds worked – they did – in those days, the audio coming from a compact disc I had burnt at home.

Looking back at the questions for that first event the line-up we went with was as follows:

> The Last 7 Days
>
> Guess the Face
>
> General Knowledge
>
> Going for a Song
>
> Food and Drink
>
> TV & Film Themes
>
> The Accumulator
>
> The Music Round
>
> A Rose By Any Other Name

Some of those rounds I knew worked well as I had used the format previously at Redwood, but some were obviously being tried for the first time. The last 7 days was topical with a mixture of news, sport, light, heavy – it allowed me to go round the audience and take away any copies of newspapers that were lying on people's tables. The very first question in the quiz was:

> 43-year-old Patricia Amos has hit the headlines this week. Why?

Typically I would write the news round with the aim that a team of six would score seven or eight out of ten. Round two was a photo round that I had at great expense copied before the wedding at a local Prontaprint. It featured photos of Kirsty Young, Gary McAllister and Mary Archer. I've no idea why, or whether they were connected. All the contestants had to do was name the face.

Round three was general knowledge, where for some reason I asked what gift would you give people on their 55th wedding anniversary. It was a bit random as I didn't know anybody who'd celebrated 50 years let alone 55, and looking at the scores for the night all the teams struggled, some only managing one correct answer.

Going for a song was a music round as you might expect, and it consisted of me playing a couple of famous lines and the audience having to name the artist and song title. "Take a sad song and make it better" was the opener. Food and drink was as the title suggests, and then we came to my personal favourite at the time which was TV and Film themes. It was a stella line-up for askTony's first commercial event Trumpton, Brookside, Ballykissangel and This Morning all featured.

Round seven was the Accumulator which was based on Who Wants To Be a Millionaire but obviously featured neither Chris Tarrant nor any money whatsoever. Instead there were ten multiple choice questions, each getting steadily harder, and the first time your team got one wrong, your scoring for the round stopped.

The penultimate round was another music round and to save time I re-used some music that had been provided for my wedding. The first dance featured, with a bit of Barry White, and there was also Caravan of Love by the Housemartins.

The final round – with the strange title of a Rose by any other Name – was anagrams of famous people on a handout.

So that was the line-up two hundred people sat down to on 16th May 2002. How did the quiz go? At the time I remember being a bit stressed, most particularly because two of my four assistants did not turn up until the start of round six. The sound system did not work particularly well, and the whole thing seemed to take ages. The quiz started just after six o-clock and we were not finished until after nine thirty.

The audience enjoyed the first round and the faces, it went a bit flat during general knowledge, picked up again during the music, got a bit competitive during the accumulator, and then completely died a death during the anagrams as the whole room went quiet. I resolved never again to try an anagrams round (a resolution I did break on occasions) and also never to do more than eight rounds as people got bored.

The fee was £500. That client never rebooked, and the only feedback I received was via one of the assistants several months later who claimed the quiz was run by a bunch of students.

However, it was not a disaster, askTony was off and running as a quiz business, and event number one had been completed.

Photo 2 The very first paid event we ran in 2002. Scruffy t-shirt.

3 AND IN SECOND PLACE

There were only two other events in 2002 following the debut in May – one in September for a law firm near Liverpool Street, and a Christmas quiz for a big multinational bank.

The law firm one was the first askTony event to be staged in a pub, in truth quite an upmarket bar/restaurant. It has a private room in a marquee style, and I was able to use all their audiovisual equipment.

This event was a bit more sophisticated than the first one in that the client wanted to eat during the quiz, and it was a bit more than bar snacks. I did the last 7 days and general knowledge before the starter, a photo and music round before the main, and then I finished off with the return of the accumulator.

A rose by any other name was the reserve round in case we had extra time – luckily, it wasn't needed.

The Christmas bank quiz passed uneventfully, and the year ended with three paid events under our belt. I charged the bank and the law firm the princely sum of £150 each for their respective quiz nights so askTony was able to declare revenues for 2002 of £800.

In early 2003 I started investigating Google Adwords and discovered that for a very small fee you could direct any search visitors who typed in quiz night direct to the askTony site via an advert that would appear on the results screen. I duly put in my credit card details and the bookings literally starting flying in.

At the time askTony was strictly a one-man band. Although later Mrs Roy was to join the business full time, I was in 2003 answering the phone, dealing with enquiries, writing the quiz nights, hosting the events, and doing some follow-ups, as well as all the marketing.

What I didn't have in 2003 was any PA equipment and so prior to event number four in March 2003 I arranged to hire one. The owner of that hire company, Gary, went on to play a pivotal part in the growth of askTony over the next four years. The event itself was a 30th birthday quiz for a banker called Henry who had attended the Christmas event. It was held in a very swish dockside restaurant and once again I judged the mood exactly right by charging exactly £100. The bill the birthday boy paid must have exceeded £5000.

Henry's quiz opened with this question:

> Which Cold Feet character was killed in Sunday's episode?

It was also the time when Charles Ingram was being accused of cheating on Who Wants To Be A Millionaire. This meant the opening to my quiz had started with a cacophony of coughing. James Gooding had also done a kiss and tell on his ex Kylie Minogue in the Sunday papers so all in all Henry picked a good week to have an "in the news round" birthday special

As Henry was celebrating the end of his third decade on the planet, the music round featured several songs from each of the decades he had been alive for. We had a bit of Frankie Goes to Hollywood mixed with some Coldplay and the unmistakable tones of Luton's very own Paul Young.

The final round was all about earnings and concentrated on the top 10 grossing film stars – specifically

> According to the Sunday Times Rich List , which British stars earned the most from starring in or directing films in 2002

On the same day askTony also provided the questions for another quiz although the hosting services were not needed. Bookings then started to come thick and fast with two big ones in April 2003 followed by a return to Redwood on May 1st. The following Friday I did an evening quiz for a professional caterer who had supplied the food for the birthday quiz, and at the end of May there was a charity event for the wife of a friend from Redwood.

June 2003 saw the first unusual venue for a quiz on board HMS President which is statically moored on the side of Thames in central London. A couple of weeks later I did a quiz for the firm my wife worked for, and that was immediately followed somewhat nepotistically by a pensions quiz for the firm my Dad worked for.

That pensions quiz was technically event sixteen and it proved memorable for several factors. The previous fifteen had all followed a similar alcohol pattern, in that as the quiz went on, and people began to relax with a few drinks, the more they seemed to enjoy it. The audience often got louder, and the format tended to fit that, with the music round staged towards the end.

At the pensions quiz despite the fact the twenty guests had been drinking solidly all evening, the individuals did not change their behaviour at all. They were all probably hardened by the daily excitement of pension forecasts with alcohol failing to loosen them.

The other strange feature was that the quiz did not start until well after 11pm making it statistically the latest quiz I've ever carried out. That is not to say it wasn't enjoyable, as the host had kindly provided a hotel room for my wife and I which we retired to shortly after 1am.

It was an early start the following morning because as well as my day job that evening was the first of a series of monthly quiz nights at a pub near Kings Cross. The fee had been agreed at £100 each month, and the venue was going to be responsible for marketing the event to get enough punters.

That first quiz was a success, and many of the same teams turned up the following month in August. As the months rolled on the owner of the pub got increasingly relaxed about publicising the event and eventually as a result only one team turned and the event was cancelled without payment. This brought an end to our association with that pub although I am pleased to say that the lack of our quiz didn't harm the business and it is thriving today with great ratings on Facebook.

This experience taught me two valuable lessons. A regular monthly quiz was hard work as you had to write completely new rounds each month, as some of the same people might turn up. The second was that payment should where possible be made in advance of the quiz, in case the organiser cancelled or changed his mind.

The bookings continued to roll in and by December 2013 we were up to event 34. This was a long drive accompanied by the wife down to Somerset for a dinner quiz booked privately by one of the guests at a previous event. It proved to be one of the least successful events.

For a start on arrival it was clear that every single one of the dozen or so guests were absolutely hammered. And possibly also under the influence of narcotics. Nobody had told us that the event was black tie, so not for the first time in my quiz night career I felt dramatically underdressed.

The Richard and Judy theme tune had proved popular in the bars of London town with the bankers, media and other groups in the months previously, but in the cold walls of the Somerset stately home the tones were as welcome as a bucket of cold sick. When the quiz was over, Karen and I slunk off back the M5 to London in the dead of night glad the client had paid upfront.

Christmas 2003 continued to be busy and the following Friday we had another romantic trip as a couple to do a quiz in deepest Suffolk. This time the Richard and Judy theme got an ecstatic reception as did a reworked version of Catchphrase which made its professional debut.

Photo 3 Wild celebrations at a 2003 event

Photo 4 A quiz for Sky early in 2004

4 KEN DODD'S DAD'S DOG IS DEAD

In just over 18 months to the end of 2003 askTony had carried out 38 events and I had learnt enough from the experience to be able to improve the business and progress in 2004. Although this did have impact on my day job.

Since leaving university in 1995 I had continued working as an internet producer but decided in the summer of 2003 to try and a career change and enrolled on a teacher training programme for a 9-month PGCE course.

This was split into three phases – a classroom based, university refresher lasting a few weeks which was good fun, a first school placement which lasted until February 2004 which proved challenging but extremely rewarding. The final phase was a second school placement which proved disastrous.

The statistics tell the whole story of that PGCE year in that of the thirty students who started in September, ranging in ages from 21 to 59 – half had dropped out by Christmas, and only nine completed the course. Two years later only one was teaching in the state sector.

Sadly I was one of the casualties as the challenging nature of the second school, the burgeoning quiz bookings, and a realisation it was a more prosperous life back in my old career, saw me pull out of the course at the beginning of March 2004.

The previous week I had carried out a quiz for the biggest brand yet. For each of the previous events I had added the client to a client list on the askTony website, but several days after this particular event having done the same thing, I had a call from their PR department to take down their name as they had a policy of not being associated with any company.

For the purposes of this book I will call that client Geoff. What was interesting about the quiz for Geoff was that the fee they paid me included the cost of the food, which I would then pay the bar for. It was just over £800 for 100 people so, after my fee was deducted, worked out at over £6 per head.

The food the venue served was an absolute disgrace and a shambles. The halftime break in the quiz arrived when we had pre-agreed with the venue that the food would be brought out. There was absolutely no sign of activity from the kitchen, or from the staff. Mrs Roy went to investigate and found the manager madly trying to unwrap frozen sausage rolls from the freezer and bung them in the microwave.

The next thirty minutes consisted of the quizmaster, his wife, and various bar staff trudging up and down about 100 concrete steps ferrying the worst type of microwave bar snacks to over hundred famished bankers. The mood turned ugly but luckily via the power of the microphone I was able to clearly communicate during the second half of the quiz just whose fault the farce had been. I was not surprised to learn the venue – which the client had selected – closed some weeks later.

The night after the bank quiz I was back in action at the other side of London hosting a quiz for Sky. This was a notable event in askTony history because just before the quiz started one of their finance team approached me and said he had built a special spreadsheet that I could use for the scoring. I looked at the sheet and it contained some of the most advanced scripting I had ever seen at the time including calculating consistency in the form of average success rate per round. It was a feature I never used but in terms of working out who was winning, it was perfect.

With some of the money coming in from quiz nights,

coupled with a return to earning decent money by going back to my day job, I invested in some key equipment for the business, some of which proved useful; others less so.

I decided askTony needed personalised clipboards so having tracked down a supplier down in Cornwall, 30 PVC boards arrived emblazoned with the askTony logo. 5,000 full-colour leaflets were produced courtesy of a company in Northamptonshire who I think miscalculated the costing as the total cost was about £25 including postage. A slave to the brand, I ordered 500 askTony pens this time with the logo reversed black on yellow. Perhaps the strangest purchase of all was 500 sticks of rock.

I was also collecting a large number of wires and connectors as in almost all the venues I had visited so far some key piece of equipment was either missing or not provided meaning a last minute panic as to whether the sound or video would work.

It was mainly the venue's televisions that could not be relied upon. Some were nailed into the wall with no SCART or HDMI connector accessible, some had screen burn having been tuned to sky sports news or equivalent for years, and some just didn't power on at all.

Even if a venue did have a competent sound system and a TV that worked, there was no guarantee it could be used for the quiz. I needed to connect my laptop to the venue sound system which was often in a completely different place to any TV screen, meaning I either had to use my own sound system, provide about fifty foot of cable to connect to the TV on the other side of the venue, or not to do any video rounds.

For this reason, I also ended up purchasing a projector and screen. This meant that for any event I could travel to the venue with a full set of kit. If the venue had stuff that worked, great – if not I could provide all my own gear, which at least had the advantage of being guaranteed to work.

For the first time in 2004 several venues asked for proof of liability insurance which was a new area for me, but quickly solved and purchased via a search on google.

One of the most useful bits of kit I bought was a ground loop isolator suggested by a manager of a London nightclub where we did a quiz event. Plugging a cheap laptop into their £50,000 sound system produced some interesting initial effects which would have pierced ear drums until a £6 cable grabbed from Amazon did the trick. It was used many times since to good effect.

To be a proper quiz company I decided askTony also needed personalised answer paper and I found a supplier in Wigan who was able to photocopy 10,000 sheets of an A4 template I sent him at a very reasonable cost of £80. Postage was a small fortune but visually it looked more impressive than plain paper and it did stop the impression created by the initial quiz that this was a bunch of students running a sloppy operation.

The 5,000 leaflets however cheap proved to be a bit of a waste as ten years later I still had about 4,900 left. Despite leaving them out at the end of events they went untouched, and I am still looking for another use for them.

A lot of the events so far had taken place in London where I lived so logistics had been reasonable straightforward. If it was a client and venue I had been to before, I could just take a laptop and a bag and turn up after my day job. If it was a brand-new venue, then I drove to work with all the equipment in my car and then headed to the event having left work early.

This approach became a little stretched in May 2004 when I had two events for BT two days apart (a Tuesday and a Thursday) in Hinckley. Luckily, I was working in Milton Keynes that week so the first event passed without problems – I jumped on the A5 shortly after 4pm having got in to work early. It was an after-dinner quiz, so I was able to set up before the guests arrived for dinner. Then it was a case of retiring to the bar before waiting to be called on to do a quick sixty-minute quiz as the guests relaxed over dessert and coffee. Job done, and the client said look forward to seeing you Thursday.

4pm Thursday poised to enact the same plan I discovered to my horror that both the M1 and A5 – the two main driving options to Hinckley were completely blocked. I parked up at Milton Keynes station, staggered onto a train to Northampton with a PA system, laptop, quiz bag and suit (luckily the venue was supplying the video) and off we chugged.

I was running late and by the time the train pulled into Northampton it must have been past six. Straight into a taxi destination Hinckley, we were way beyond the scheduled arrival time. I got to the hotel just as the guests were discreetly tucking away a prawn cocktail starter. A setup under subterfuge and eventually the quiz passed off like clockwork. But undeniably a stressful prelude, and the taxi bill both from and to the station wiped out any profit.

The bill for the two BT events was exactly £517 and so I was slightly surprised a few weeks later when the company bank account was credited with £5170. Perhaps that is what the client felt the evening was worth.

Towards the summer of 2004 I did a little bit of research into the competition. On the google page of results that came up when you typed quiz night we noticed a company called Quiz Quiz Quiz. It looked a slick operation with several quiz masters and a range of existing clients. A friend put in an anonymous enquiry and found that they were charging roughly double our fee. I got a group together to attend an event they were running at a pub in west London. It was a good quiz although there were certain differences with our events. First, the questions were all mixed with no set rounds, and secondly the marking all seemed to take place at the end. Reassured that competition was healthy, I could charge more, and that our format was if not better, certainly a differential, I left the quiz and returned to concentrate on askTony.

Bookings were coming in thick and fast and between the

BT events in May and the end of the year there were another thirty askTony quiz nights including the first ever one to leave the mainland.

A financial company in Jersey had been in contact in the summer and requested a quiz on the principality. A quick google of air fares and likely costs had led me to quote a world record fee of £795 knowing that it would also necessitate two days holiday from work.

On the 4th November 2004 a day before Mr. Fawkes tried unsuccessfully to blow up the mother of parliaments, Mr. Roy landed in Jersey to bring quiz entertainment to a group of 100 or so financiers. As befits an astronomical fee I had come up with what I believed to be a stellar line-up. We kicked off with in the news, followed up with a photo round, then general knowledge, then a bit of TV themes still featuring Richard and Judy. After the break a relatively new round – The Price Is Right – where users had to guess the price of ten specially selected secondhand cars. Film themes had been mixed for the evening with some Countdown conundrums, then we climaxed with a music round and a mystery round wipeout.

Wipeout was another popular TV quiz show with the late great Paul Daniels. Contestants had to name the ten correct answers from a grid also containing some wrong answers. If a muggle selected a wrong answer you can guess what happened.

On paper in Jersey this translated to working out which of the twenty cities I had typed out had staged a summer Olympics. It proved a successful end to the quiz and a rebooking for the following year was promised. The next week I was back in London Town for a first event for an estate agency near Victoria. This too proved successful and the start of several annual events for that client. Towards the end of November, I was at the microphone for an event in St Albans and prepared for a life-changing December.

For all the events that took place there were another few

that never materialised. There was great excitement for a few weeks when we were approached to carry out a quiz for a London museum. The excitement was due to receiving total confirmation that the quiz would be hosted by Barry from Eastenders. A lot of other details were missing however and in the event the quiz never happened – or at least it did not take place with our involvement.

Another one that got away was for a television production company who were after a quiz for their company away day. The unusual aspect of this quiz was the client wanted it to take place on board a train from Euston to Liverpool. Originally I was quite keen but after a few clarifications it emerged the guests would not have been sat together, and I decided the logistics would be a nightmare. There was also quite a lot going on elsewhere in my life and I could have done without the aggravation.

In the first week of December 2004 I accepted a job with the BBC, my wife gave birth to our first child, and there was a quiz event the following night somewhere in south London. It was an unusual event in that it took place on a Saturday night in the client's offices. They were an exceedingly small computer firm and on arrival it looked as though the atmosphere would be completely absent but a few cheap drinks later from Tesco and there was a bit of karaoke during the lyrics round.

The following week as I was leaving my current job anyway, I managed to take some time off to carry out quiz nights on four consecutive nights starting on the Tuesday. That night I was in Leicester, then it was back to London for three more, all using the same material. Technically as almost all my quiz nights take place on work nights it was five quiz nights in five working days as there was another event on the Monday which proved to be the final event of the year.

There were 46 events in total in 2004 taking the overall figure since that first post-wedding event to 85. Little was I to know, about to start a new job for the world's greatest broadcaster, that the overall figure was to double in the next twelve months, I was to work with a quiz mastering legend, and we were to receive our first complaint.

Photo 5 Making friends after the Jersey quiz in 2004

5 CUNNING STUNTS

2005 dawned with Steve Brookstein hitting the top of the charts fresh from the success of winning ITV's The X Factor. For askTony the first event of the year was a hotel quiz with a golf theme for a client associated with that sport. The venue was Oulton Hall near Leeds which turned out to be a very swish hotel but a long, long drive from London. Considering it was a week night and a very late finish the price I charged was ridiculously steep, but I was pleased that askTony had started to burst out of the London bubble and was attracting big clients from around the UK.

My start date at the BBC was the following week and the only quiz event in that week was a local one in the city of London. It was for a bank who became a regular askTony client over the next ten years often hosting several events a year for their staff. I had a friend from university who kindly offered to help me, and the quiz once again featured the Richard & Judy theme tune which I was still flogging to death.

That client introduced me to a game which was to become a staple of some quizzes in the future called True or False. This required a series of true or false questions. There are several variations but in this one, if the audience member thinks the statement is true, they put their hands on the head. If they think it is false, their hands go on their bum. If they are wrong, they sit down.

The game continues until either Christmas arrives, or there is one person left standing. It was suggested to me at the end of the quiz for the bank that I should run this game next time, and as the same client decided to rebook for April, it was an idea that I took up.

Thinking about it at home that weekend I decided the hands-on head version would not work in a lot of the venues I had been to, as it would not be immediately clear who was still left in. I printed out 100 sheets with a big T on blue paper and 100 sheets with a big F on yellow. I then realised that for these sheets to be reusable I was going to need to laminate them. A quick trip to Staples secured the necessary equipment, although I could perhaps have done with investing slightly more in a faster device, as each sheet took several minutes to preserve.

Still, it gave the mother in law something to do on her visit the following weekend.

That bank quiz took place in what was fast becoming one of my favourite venues, a pub just Cheapside that specialised in pizzas. Not only did it have a dedicated upstairs area available for hire for free, but for around £6 a head the chef knocked out decent pizzas from his special ovens. Given experiences so far in similar London pubs had been exclusively "microwave it all" variants, this made for a refreshing change.

There was time for one more quiz in January for my old company Redwood, before another hotel event this time in the faded grandeur of Sutton Coldfield. This was a dinner quiz which the client had instructed to take place squarely between the hours of 9.30pm and 11pm. My experience so far of hotel quizzes was that timings very rarely held. Often the client would arrive for dinner late, meaning the hotel schedule was knocked, resulting in the quiz being delayed.

For these type of events provided the logistics worked out, I would try and arrive before the guests sat down, set up my equipment, and then disappear to the bar to wait for the call from the hotel manager or client to be told the guests were ready.

As it turned out the Sutton event stuck pretty much exactly to the schedule I was given, and I drove back down the M6 / M1 to London reflecting on the fact I was beginning to clock up the motorway miles. It was a similar story a couple of weeks later as I found myself heading to one of the top hotels in the country at Pennyhill Park in Bagshot. The event had required quite a lot of preparation as the client had sent over some special audio and video questions on a CDROM. I was sufficiently impressed with the venue to book an anniversary night for Karen and myself.

I was living in East London, and working in West London, so at the time an event like the one in Guildford at a pub for quite a small company didn't prove too tough to get to. But I preferred London venues as it meant a lot could be done via public transport. Particularly when askTony was approaching another landmark – two events on the same night. For this I obviously needed a second quizmaster.

I explained the problem to my right-hand man Gary who had provided PA equipment and he offered to give quiz hosting a go.

On the 9th March 2005 askTony stepped into the unknown with yours truly at an event in the city in a South African pub, with Gary on the other side of London hosting a hotel quiz for some managers at a charity. My event went well although I was surprised to find the client had separately booked a man to provide karaoke straight after the quiz. This resulted in us both bringing our own sound systems, which given the venue also had a full DJ booth looked like a bit of overkill.

Thankfully Gary passed his first quizmaster outing with flying colours with the client reporting great feedback. This had been helped according to Gary by them all being steaming drunk early on in proceedings. The following night I was back out in the country at the magnificent Hartwell Manor hotel near Aylesbury. Here I was greeted by a client who was awfully specific in his requests just before I picked up the mike to start the quiz. We had been booked for a 9.30 start, but it was 10pm before the thirty guests were ready, although the chief was adamant the quiz had to finish by 11pm. It finished twelve seconds before the deadline which earned the respect of the management.

There were three more events; a quiz in a Liverpool Street pub, a trip back on the M4 to Slough for a big name in paints, and an event at the offices of prestigious London lawyers, before another landmark in askTony history. Our first ever complaint.

Looking back this was all entirely my fault. It was the evening of the 7th April 2015 and we again had a double booking. There was a quiz in Tower Bridge in a pub specialising in pizza (not that one) for a non-profit that was only ten minutes from my flat. Or there was a hotel quiz in the middle of the Midlands for a well-known bank. Gary drew the short straw and got the bank. It proved to be a mistake.

The Tower Bridge quiz went down well with 19 teams, great pizza, and a celebrity price is right round which involved guessing how much a particular celebrity cost to hire for the night. The idea had come to me for an enquiry we had received as to whether we could provide a quiz with a celebrity quiz master. It turned out we could providing the client had very big pockets. At that time the cheapest celebrity we could find was Jimmy White the snooker player costing £2,000 plus expenses.

Gary meanwhile was having a nightmare on the M40 and got to the quiz a couple of hours later than scheduled. As the event was a post dinner affair this was not disastrous. In his post-event debrief the following day he said the actual quiz went OK although he had some difficulty in leaving as the assistant he had brought to help him was having a few drinks with the client.

A few days later I got an email from the client as follows:

> I can only express extreme disappointment at your representatives on-site behaviour and execution of the quiz. The quiz delivery lacked lustre

- whilst the photos depict an engaged audience, I would say that during visits to check on the proceedings, it looked very ordinary, guests were not as enamoured as the photos project. Secondly, I would expect professional conduct of personnel from all our suppliers and would bring the following to your attention:

Events staff do not socialise with clients on -site. Rationale for this golden rule is that our conferences/meetings are primarily a team building exercise, welcoming new members to the business unit for networking opportunities/discussions in a relaxed environment. I am amazed that one of your team would stay post event to socialise - especially given the other had made it perfectly clear that he was ready to leave - and was waiting for about an hour to do so.

It sounded as though during the quiz some of the guests had taken a shine to the assistant and invited her to stay for a few drinks afterwards. Unusually the complainant had not actually been at the quiz but popping in to observe every now and again.

I sent a long reply by email:

Thanks for your email and feedback. Firstly, I'd like to apologise for the disappointment you felt with our performance on the evening. I can honestly say that with over 80 events in less than 18 months, this is the first complaint we have had from a client, and as such I take it very seriously.

The explanation I have had from the quizmaster was that the assistant felt she should stay for drinks as she had been requested to by a number of the guests. Their thinking was had the assistant refused these requests, your guests could have been offended and tarnished their view of the quiz.

We are often invited to have a drink after the quiz has finished, which we generally accept as it often gives us an opportunity to find out how the quiz was received.

I am very keen to prove to you that askTony values professional service very highly, and would very much like another opportunity to demonstrate this - we can offer all sorts of quiz events, and I can supply references from satisfied clients across many sectors – including television, legal, the public sector and banking.

I am so confident we can meet your expectations I will offer you another hosted quiz to your requirements and specification free of charge *. The only pledge I ask for is that if you are satisfied you use us for a quiz again.

The client did not take me up on that offer, but we did work with the same company again, albeit a different department. Perhaps not surprisingly despite annually declaring profits in the billions it took the same client over two months to pay for that event, a record for slow payment that still stands to this day.

The complaint quiz was statistically number 100 and there was no time to sit back and reflect as April 2005 proved to be the busiest month so far with eleven events. One evening I was in Broadgate Circle inside company premises for a quiz that had been several months in the making. The two client contacts seemed to know each other well but also did not seem to agree. I would get a call or email from the man with an instruction, only for it to be reversed a few days later by his colleague.

When I met the couple on the night all was revealed as it turned out not only were they colleagues in the office, they were also lovers in the night (and possibly the daytime as well). There were a few technical problems during the quiz including no sound on the film round. My equipment was exonerated, and it was a situation I was increasingly finding – despite a lot of these firms having luxurious offices, their conference equipment was often seriously lacking, with this office being no different.

The month finished with a Saturday night quiz for an exclusive sports club in West London. This was the start of a ten-year relationship with the club where the welcome was always incredibly friendly. The format remained the same as on that first night. We would have four rounds of quiz action, then the guests would disappear upstairs for a buffet of lasagna or chilli, followed by another four rounds from about 9.30 or 10pm.

It was an exclusive club with some high-powered guests, a fact I became aware of at that first quiz when I unveiled the Price Is Right round. Guests had to identify the price of an item following a short TV style introduction voiced by me with some photos of the product. I had carried out the round before with some success, and as I liked to select a variety of products to suit the typical quiz audience, I often used that bible of home shopping, the Argos catalogue. There might be something for the gardeners, something technological, a piece of home furnishing, and maybe even a speedboat in a nod to Bullseye.

As I was unveiling the answers to the London crowd, a sophisticated voice piped up from the back with the words: "Darling, I doubt anyone here has even set foot in Argos let alone bought anything". For that client in future I took due note and swapped it for John Lewis items.

After a break of a few weeks I was next back in quiz action

in Hammersmith in the final week of May 2005. The venue was a pub which four years earlier had hosted a raucous hen night for an uncontrollable group of ladies including my wife-to-be. It all smacked of being incredibly low-budget and tacky, although the quiz was nothing of the sort, and the drinks company went home happy.

It was an unusually busy summer as there was still quiz action through June and July including a dinner event at a top London hotel for a betting company. This quiz went down in askTony history.

For most of the events so far we had been quite relaxed about asking for food and drink to be provided for the quiz-master. A drink was often offered, and there might be a couple of chicken wings or sandwiches from the buffet, but here the client spared no expense.

The guests were all eating a 3-course meal before the quiz took place, and I arranged for a similar meal to be served for myself and two assistants. There was also a couple of bottles of wine. As a result, I have almost no memory of the actual quiz, except one of the assistants became fairly friendly with a guest during the music round, which continued for several months after the event had finished.

As the autumn started there was a great excitement at askTony headquarters which had newly relocated to London Luton after our house move from Whitechapel. We received an enquiry from a marketing agency asking for six quiz nights for a car firm to be held across the country in October. This was then followed a week later with a request for a grand final to take place in Birmingham.

The negotiations were quite complex, and it was our biggest booking to date. Karen was dispatched to the marketing company's offices in Oxford to seal the deal. The first event was to take place in a pub near Crawley at the start of October.

There was time before that for a quick trip to Edinburgh on the 23rd September for a bank quiz. I also placed an order for a buzzer system from the United States as I was worried my quiz nights were needing to become more technologically sophisticated. Another purchase saw 100 black quiz champions mugs arrive as the marketing budget got extended once again, together with a pack of oversized giant playing cards. This was to allow a round called Play Your Cards Right, which I ended up using once in the next ten years.

On October 3rd I set off for Crawley for the first of a six night tour of the UK that saw thirty guests from the same firm compete in the regional heats. The winning team each night qualified for the grand final. After Crawley it was Peterborough a couple of days later, than across to Bath the following night. I then diverted to Daventry for a big conference quiz for an IT company, before hitting the road for a big drive the next week with heat four in Stirling. There then followed a hop south the next day to Warrington. We finished in York on October 13th.

News came through the following week that the quiz final would be hosted by the great Roy Walker, the Catchphrase legend who had been enjoying a radio resurgence thanks to Chris Moyles on Radio 1 where he had voiced a segment called Carpark Catchphrase.

The night before I was back in Jersey for a return visit to the financial company who had booked the year before. This time there was not much chance for drunken shenanigans on plastic cows that had accompanied the year before. I was straight on a plane back to East Midlands for a trip over to the Birmingham Marriot hotel where we were due to meet up with Roy.

The client had asked for the final questions to be sent well in advance so Roy could study them on the cruise he was currently on. We arrived early in Birmingham and ran into another legend on approach to the hotel when Ken Dodd walked past. He was appearing in his one man show at a theatre up the road.

When we met up with the other legend shortly after 5pm

it turned out that was the first time Roy had seen the questions, but it didn't matter as like a true professional he mastered any difficult pronunciations.

The clients, Roy, my assistant, and I enjoyed a good meal before the quiz, and we then practiced the introduction Roy wanted to get the guests bouncing. As I was not in my usual role with the microphone, I would effectively be running the quiz technicalities, with Roy the front man. As a result, I had once again badly misjudged the dress code and turned up for the biggest event of my career in a very scruffy ensemble. It was a repeat of that first event when we were mistaken for students.

Roy made me repeat the warm-up for the guests until I finally put the right amount of energy into it, and just after 8pm seven teams competing in the grand final heard the words:

"Ladies and Gentlemen, it is that time you have all been waiting for. Here he is, the legend behind Carpark Catchphrase – it is time for you to say what you see – here he is – it is R – O – Y   W -A-L-K-E-R!"

The audience loved it and Roy ran on stage (or more accurately straight from the bathroom through the connecting door of the Marriot) into the conference room. He did a little warm-up and then flew through the quiz with no major alarms. When it was time to declare the winners, he stayed behind afterwards to sign papers, photos, and even a few breasts.

I learnt a lot from working with Roy for those few short hours. He told me that no matter how few guests were in the audience, he always insisted on using a microphone. This was partly to save his voice, and to ensure he could always talk over any hecklers should he need to.

An absolute gentleman, Roy then insisted on having a drink with us at the bar before we headed off and left him to continue partying with the guests. The following day I headed off a day trip to France with the family completing an exhausting but memorable forty-eight hours in askTony history. With 18 completed quiz nights in the calendar month, October 2005 again broke the record as the busiest in our short history.

Several new clients in 2005 went on to become regular askTony clients over the next ten years. Next stop after the excitement of Roy Walker was a trip to a well-known car company just outside Slough, followed by a trip to Beckenham for a big name in client services. That event took place under the watchful eye of Margaret Thatcher whose portrait hung just outside the gentlemen's toilets, taking place as it did in the town's conservative club.

That Beckenham quiz was always the most challenging of the events I staged for a few reasons. Firstly, the drive took ages. If I left from work, I had to negotiate the South Circular, which was usually grid-locked. If I left from Luton, there were various options, but they all took an eternity. So I would usually arrive frazzled.

Secondly, there were normally about thirty-five teams. This required at least a couple of helpers to mark the papers. Thirdly although the venue had a stage at the front and plenty of seating, the management also let in regular punters who sat near the bar and took no part in the quiz. So it was pretty difficult to work out who was participating and who was not.

The technology was a fourth problem. The PA system had been installed in the sixties by the looks of it and was situated right at the back of the room, a good hundred metres from the stage area. There was a projector above the stage. This left only two viable options. One was to stand on the stage with a laptop, and use your own sound system. Or you could stand at the back near their in-house version, and not do any video rounds.

There was another first for askTony at the start of December when I travelled to a chateau just outside Paris for a bank quiz. This event had easily the highest budget of any quiz so far with the winners showered with gifts that must have run into several thousands. As with the betting quiz, the food and drink provided were superb, and it proved a fitting way to end the most successful year to date.

That bank quiz had to quite carefully constructed as barely any of the guests had English as their first language. But after a number of conversations we were able to settle on an international format that satisfied the client, and the evening passed off without a hitch. It was a hugely impressive venue and if you are lucky enough ever to be in the Chantilly area check out Chateau de Montvillargenne.

So many events, a day job, and quite a bit of travel did lead up to an interesting situation at a bank quiz in Canary Wharf in one of the final events of the year. I was tired and arrived at the venue for the pre-quiz checks about 5pm.

It was a Thursday and the quiz was set for a relatively early 6pm start so I was planning to be out of there by 9pm and home early. I met up with the client who was on crutches. All was going well until she asked what time I would be likely to start the karaoke.

There was no karaoke. On exceedingly rare occasions a couple of clients had asked us to play a bit of music after the quiz finished, but in general the booking terms were always clear that our involvement ended when the quiz finished. Most venues anyway had their own music or DJ who would come in after the quiz, so this was never a problem.

I explained to the lady in question that there was no karaoke booked, and she was not happy. There was a slightly heated conversation which ended with her hobbling back to the office to ring the askTony bookings manager. She had to go back to her desk to get the number. I did not feel like telling her she could have my wife's number or call her on my phone.

I did start to pack up the equipment in a bit of a strop but was persuaded to stay. The quiz went well and by the end of the event I did apologise for the confusion over the microphone and I think all was forgiven.

In addition to the events we did host, Karen was also dealing with a number of enquiries that also led nowhere. A lady had been in contact wanting a bar mitzvah quiz for her son. It was for 100 people including a dozen teenagers and a key stipulation was that guests could move around easily during the quiz. We never heard from the lady again.

Zoe called in to say she had arranged an away day for her SMT and Heads of Department in Preston. A quick google revealed she was referring to her Senior Management Team with that TLA. Her three-letter acronym. She would like a Monday evening and was keen on a music quiz to take place after dinner. A private dining room had been arranged and numbers would be limited to 17. Our estimate proved too high.

A mobile firm was in touch with the correspondent very keen on a round purely about telephones. They also insisted a joker round be used where the numbers one to ten were presented before each round and the round score multiplied by that number. To make it more interesting a further suggestion was that the numbers be in Armenian.

The Canary Wharf karaoke fiasco event did illustrate that as fast as askTony was growing in terms of bookings, and the events kept rolling in, it did not take much to send me a bit on edge. It was not surprising really as the year closed with a record 87 events taking place in the 12 months, more than the previous 3 years put together.

Photo 6 Big dinner quiz with proper staging in 2005

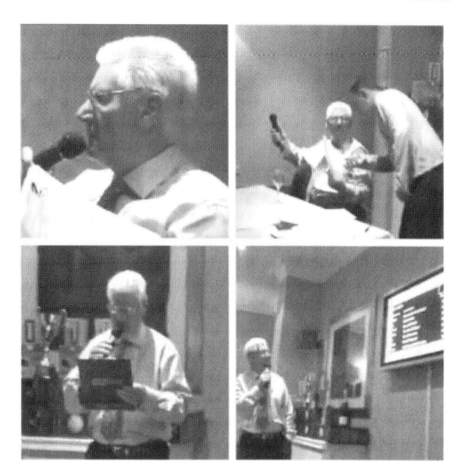

Photo 7 - A blurry montage of the great Roy Walker hosting an ask-Tony quiz night in 2005

6 WHOSE ROUND IS IT ANYWAY

The early months of 2006 saw several trips to the north. But first there was an event in Docklands as part of the London boat show. This was an unusual quiz for askTony as it was open to the general public. As such I was unable to prepare in the normal way.

With a quiz for a company, you can ask for a profile of the audience. Typically, these questions include how many men, how many women, any international guests, age range, and sometimes job function. From these answers you can construct a quiz that appeals to a broad cross-section of the audience. You can slip in a few tunes from the eighties if the guests are in their 30s or 40s. If the audience is all graduates in their twenties, old television theme tunes would be a bit pointless.

For the boat quiz however I did not know a) how many members of the public would turn up, and b) any aspect of their demographic profile. As it turned out, I also had to battle a venue that was not set up for hosting a quiz night.

The pub was vast on two floors, and there were no private areas. The organiser of the quiz had not booked a specific part of the venue, so I set the quiz up with my own equipment in the upstairs corner. Slowly guests came trickling in, but they sat interspersed with members of the public who had absolutely no interest in any quiz questions. So as the quiz got underway, it was difficult to work out who was in the quiz and who was not.

A stressful ninety minutes later, the quiz closed, and the three teams who managed to participate each managed to get a prize as the organiser was expecting many more teams. As I drove away, I was thankful askTony did not have to deal with public quiz nights and decided that boat quiz would probably be the last of its type.

February saw a couple of events for the same building firm. One was staged at their southern headquarters in Bedfordshire, and the second was for their northern branch just outside Manchester. The events were two days apart and although I did not re-use any questions, it did allow me to have some quite good banter with the Manchester audience. At regular intervals I chided the Mancunians that their Bedfordshire colleagues had consistently outscored them. The truth however was the reverse

In the spring I headed back north again for a quiz close to my heart. The client had asked for an entire quiz about sport. The venue was the Sports Café in Leeds. Arriving at the venue, I had a lot of trouble connecting to their video system and it emerged we were going to have play the AV rounds from a machine in their kitchen that was curiously wired to the venue's plasma screens. .

Looking back the questions I asked were a bit odd. We started with a photo round on screen accompanied by some national anthems. The guests had to identify the country whose anthem was playing, and the completely unrelated sports personality. So Argentina was matched with Paula Radcliffe. A grinning Freddie Flintoff appeared on screen to the tune of the Ghanaian melody. Round two was a selection of ten goals I had cut together; the audience had to identify the goal scorer. Because the scorer was in vision, this was an easy round and would have worked better if I had just played the radio commentary.

Round three was general sports knowledge. Round four, after a short food break, was another helping of Tony's great goals (a continuation from the second round). Round five was

51

probably the best of the night; a selection of sports clips featuring famous action. The teams had to identify the year the action took place.

I had used a similar format in previous events featuring news items, and it always generated quite good conversation in a team as there was almost always someone in the audience who had a particular memory of the year involved.

The final round was based on family fortunes and featured the top five words people associated with football. Again, this format I had used before. I always introduced this round by saying I personally had interrogated one hundred people that morning in whichever town or city I was in.

The second and final question in the family fortunes round asked the audience to name the five favourites to be the next England football manager as of 10.30 that morning. The answers were O'Neill, Allardyce, Taylor, Curbishley and Hiddink. So it was a surprise when several weeks later Steve McLaren got the gig.

I negotiated the trip north with no problem and the elderly Vauxhall holding up well. It was a different story a week later when I set off from home to do a local quiz at a school parents association about twenty miles away.

Driving up the hill out of Luton on a hot summer afternoon I was aware of a bump. I obviously was not concentrating totally because a few minutes later, just before the roundabout that leads to the motorway, several cars started to flash me. I looked behind and realised that my car boot was open.

I pulled over and walked round the back to shut the boot. It was only then that I realised not only had the boot opened as I had driven up the hill, but the bump I heard was the sound system falling out of the back. I put in a panic call back to base and headed back down the hill to see if I could retrieve the system. There was no sign of it.

About an hour later I arrived at the venue and explained that my sound system had got lost in transit. It emerged that the venue already had their own PA speaker they used for sports sessions. The quiz went ahead, passed off successfully, and on my return home I put in an order for a replacement.

The only equipment I needed a couple of weeks later was my own laptop. The event was a film quiz for a consulting firm in the city of London. The client had hired their own sound and video system, featuring several projectors and screens, and numerous speakers. All I was required to do was turn up and do the quiz, wearing black tie.

It was an Oscars themed night so there was red carpet for the guests, and plenty of food and drink. I was slightly spooked when talking to the venue's manager a few minutes before the start. He told me that the two paintings at either end of the room were worth several million pounds. He added that they were protected by a laser system, and if anyone touched either painting the sirens would go off and police would arrive in an instant.

I spent the whole quiz worried that now I had this information I would casually rest against one of the pictures, reach up and touch it. Thankfully that did not happen, and the quiz passed off very successfully. The guests left fortified by plenty of alcohol and some great nosh. Unfortunately, there was a bitter postscript as several months later I received an invoice from the client for a sandwich that had been provided to me at halftime in the quiz. At £16 it proved to be an expensive two slices of buttered bread.

Late June saw a quiz with an international flavour staged at a country hotel. The organiser had been extremely helpful prior to the quiz and specified exactly what she wanted:

> The ages of the delegates vary between 30 and 60 years old of varying nationalities including English, German, American, Singaporean, Chinese (HK), South African, Welsh. The main objective for us of the quiz is for our global teams to cross the cultural divide and 'bond'. We don't all know each other very well (have met a few times before) so

I am hoping it will be fun and bring the Teams together. It will therefore be important to have a good balance in the questions for all the nationalities. We will be about 24 people and will be divided into 4/5 teams or so. Once you have had a thought on this, please send me your suggested questions etc. for me to have a look. Also, I think it might be fun to intersperse the rounds throughout the dinner and not to wait until dessert. Sometimes these dinners are a struggle and it would be good to get things going with some 'entertainment' before it's over, so perhaps a music round or something - not sure if this is unorthodox, so what are your thoughts?

The event went brilliantly not least because it was one of those rare occasions when a plate of sandwiches had been pre-ordered for me, so I didn't start the quiz starving. I went with a mega-safe internationally friendly line-up that included five world news questions, some photos of world leaders, a geography round featuring countries underneath the equator, some incredibly easy movie clips, and a universal music round where you just had to name the song. For some reason I did spend most of the evening bantering with the German guest. Looking at the date this was probably connected to the World Cup which was going on at the time. The offended German approached me at the end of the quiz and was very vocal in expressing the view that I had a tremendous problem with his nation. The client did not mind, and it was perhaps the best audience feedback at a quiz I had ever had. Although a few days later I did get a nice note:

Thanks for the quiz - it was great and thanks for the photos perhaps just a minor word - I know you asked whether the jokes about Germany were a problem and I said no; on reflection, perhaps it is safer to tease the English when on home ground. other than that, it was fantastic and very entertaining. thanks for your effort.

Events in the summer slowed down a bit, although there was time for an audience that I was worried would prove a bit intimidating. It was an after-dinner event comprising thirty headmasters and headmistresses. Thankfully they proved quite receptive to my mixture of fairly low-brow questions and were a good-natured group.

At the start of September askTony had a challenging booking to carry out a quiz on the Thames for a publishing company. The instructions were to board the vessel at Greenwich. The complication was the client wanted video and there were no facilities on board. I had already established that my usual projector and screen would not be viable given the restricted space. As I pulled into Greenwich that day, I had a 32 inch TV from home in the boot.

The problem was it was impossible to park anywhere close to the dock. I eventually got into a public car park and then had to stagger at least a mile to load all the stuff onto the boat. A journey I had to then repeat with the television.

The guests all got on and it was clear they had already had a few drinks. The boat trip was choppy, and the television was perched precariously on the bannister between a set of stairs. Luckily, it lasted for the duration, and the guests seemed to enjoy the quiz. Returning to Greenwich several hours later still a bit sick from the motion of the boat, I resolved that would be askTony's first and last quiz on water.

As winter drew in, I found myself at opposite ends of the country. At the beginning of October, I was in Brighton for a government department. The following week I went to a lovely hotel near St Andrews to do an after-dinner quiz for a well-known bank.

Two events in December stood out. First it was another

trip north, this time to Sheffield for a Christmas quiz for a university. I needed to get back to London the following day for work, so I took the decision to go up on the train with my still relatively new replacement sound system.

I had booked one of Sheffield's cheapest and worst hotels, but it was convenient for the venue. It also allowed me to walk past the prestigious Crucible Theatre, home of the world snooker tournament that I had watched every year in my youth. It was a mistake not to have taken a taxi from the station to the hotel as it was a walk almost entirely uphill.

I was on the 0615 from Sheffield station the next morning, so it was an incredibly early departure from the hotel. There was still time to be chased by a homeless man outside the station who claimed I had been looking at him the wrong way. Boarding the train there was no respite, as the buffet car had run out of bacon rolls. I did question the train manager about this, as I was unclear how the train could have run out when it had only just departed Sheffield which was where the train started.

Several weeks later, on Christmas Day itself, I set off from Luton for Bournemouth for a hotel quiz that had been booked several months before. It has caused much discussion in the family as to whether it was a booking we should have accepted, as it would mean disrupting the family Christmas. The money was good though, so it was not really something we were going to turn down.

I left Luton at 4pm after an alcohol-free Christmas lunch. The thing that strikes you about driving on Christmas Day is that there are no lorries on the road. This makes it a lot quicker to get anywhere. I was in Bournemouth just after 6pm and introduced myself to the hotel manager.

The quiz had been booked as a way of entertaining the guests who were staying in the hotel for their Christmas break. They had all had a good lunch and several other bits of entertainment had been put on. The quiz was the final piece of the jigsaw.

The hotel had provided a great room, which comfortably held at least two hundred people. As it turned out, there were only eight teams for the quiz and about forty people in total. Some teams consisted of elderly grandparents, others were family groups, and there was one containing two childless couples.

This quiz was like the boat quiz that had opened the year in that once again I had no idea who would turn up, and what age they would be. I was able to make certain assumptions based on prejudices about the type of people who spend Christmas in a hotel.

We opened with a news round based on events of the year which went down OK. The second round was a photo round with various celebrities all separately obscured by a Santa hat and beard. I dropped the general knowledge thinking it would be a bit dull for 9pm on Christmas night. Instead we had tv themes, a film round, and some upbeat pop intros that guests had to guess.

The final round was a special Christmas edition of family fortunes. First people had to guess something that people do on Christmas morning. The second question was something people break. I liked that question because answer four was wind, and it always raised a chuckle.

That did not happen on this particular evening, and a quiz that had started out with a ray of festive cheer climaxed in almost silence. I drove out of Bournemouth on the deserted roads to continue my Christmas holiday. Christmas Day quizzes were consigned like boat quizzes to the askTony dusty bin.

Various events did not happen in 2006 despite early promising signs. A man representing a supermarket wanted two quizzes on different nights and had a budget of £1,000 per night. However they wanted to reserve £900 of that purely for prizes. His previous supplier had cruelly not provided a music round so that was a must.

Antonia from a north London borough got in touch and

seemed very happy with our standard 8-round format. A price was agreed, an invoice was generated, the venue was booked, and a date confirmed. 10 days before the event Antonia was back in touch with a cancellation as not enough people were interested.

Emma contacted us via the website with an enquiry that proved to be achingly familiar in future years:

> We are an event management company putting together a proposal for a charity event to be held in London this October for 200 guests. The theme of the quiz will be Popular Culture and we will have 20 teams of 10. The quiz will take place in two halves, one before dinner and one after, and we would like it to be as interactive as possible, for example with video clips, mimes, name that tune, feel the sportsman (or similar), buzzer rounds etc. We would also if possible like to use good technology for the event and do away with pieces of paper with computerised scoring.

Alarm bells sounded at the words "event management company" representing a charity. Whatever price we quoted, the event management company would then stick their percentage on, which would then have to go a charity to get sign off. Emma got back in touch to say that Roy Walker had agreed to host the occasion, but sadly after that the trail went dead and the event never materialised.

A newspaper group notorious for bad spelling got in touch to ask about an event in Harrogate for 170 people. Details were sketchy:

> Our brief is very loose at the moment. We have been sponsoring an event for a few years but have decided to change the format and are looking at the possibility of a quiz. The event has been a real

success in past years so we are anxious that the new event be very slick in terms on planning and execution.

All I can say for sure at the moment is that: The quiz will be a post dinner event at a 3 day conference and will be followed by a disco We will be using a production company to dress the room We are looking for the quiz to last around 1.5 hours with a short (10min?) interval We are undecided on themes so are completely open to suggestions at the moment.

I travelled across to their offices for a rare face-to-face client meeting. The tone proved to be fairly patronising and I left with the impression they were going to interrogate various companies and then probably chose the cheapest.

A well-known recruitment firm wanted an event in Westminster for 60 people. Their venue did not have any equipment, so we were to bring it all. Negotiations had been going well until it came to price. Their budget? £70.

Alcoholics Anonymous wanted to stage a quiz in Chelmsford following an all-day convention. Again, budget proved to be an issue. A man called Steve wanted us to create a quiz for his wedding. Turned out there would be no music or dancing at the entire wedding so we decided being the sole entertainment would be too much pressure.

A quiz we probably did well to avoid was one requested by Chris being staged at Old Trafford Cricket ground. 150 people were attending and our quote of £695 was deemed excessive. In the event the client booked Stuart Hall for a fee considerably higher.

Despite these rejections 2006 had seen us host another 97 events, beating the 2005 figure. There was no sign of slowing down.

Photo 8 Excitement building during the True and False round in 2006

7 AND IN SECOND PLACE

January 2007 was another record breaker in that we did more events in January than any year before. The first was a return to the pizza pub in the City for the debut of a round called famous paintings. Several paintings were shown on screen and the guests had to work out the artist. In a cunning variation, there were then some paintings shown on screen, and the contestants had to name the picture title once I had told them the artist. The round did not really work, every team got full marks, and I never used the format again.

The second event was a quiz that took up an entire weekend. The event itself barely lasted an hour, but it was the drive there and back that took ages. It was a journey into the depths of Snowdonia. I made good progress down the M4 and had cracked the Welsh border, but it then seemed to take another several hours before I arrived. The venue was a delightful place but far too expensive for a humble quiz master to stay in, so I was five minutes down the road in a very bleak bed and breakfast that cost about £18. For that price it was a surprise to find an actual bed included but obviously with no sign of breakfast the next morning, I was back on the road early for home.

January still had not finished and after my Welsh trip it was up to Manchester next for a quiz in a prominent city centre hotel. The same company had two offices and once the northern leg was over, it was a trip south to Milton Keynes to deal with the other branch.

Positively coining in the motorway miles, the month finally ended with a memorable quiz for a university in Birmingham. I arrived at the campus for an unusual start time, 11am. I did not have all that many details in terms of what to expect, so was nonetheless surprised to discover the audience consisted of just eight staff members.

Now all the quiz nights up until this point had assumed a minimum number of teams taking part. I think the lowest up until Birmingham had been about three teams with fifteen people in total. That still managed to generate a bit of friendly competitive atmosphere, although at the time did not really justify my use of a 200 watt PA system to speak through.

Being 11am I was resigned to the fact the quiz was almost guaranteed to be completely dry. Without alcohol to fuel the contestants, it was left to me to arrange the eight brave souls into two groups of four. My usual format of eight rounds was over in about forty-five minutes, so I had to invent a few extra games to fill the two hours the client had booked. At one point I completely ran out of ideas and grabbed the flipchart that was abandoned at the back, and we had an impromptu game of win, lose or draw.

The organiser had warned me that one of the eight contestants would not take part in the quiz due to certain personality issues. So really, I was left with seven less than receptive individuals to try and generate two hours entertainment without alcohol. I left the university just after 1pm extremely glad to get out, and not entirely sure why we had been booked.

There was also time in January to visit the Midland Hotel in Manchester city centre for a dinner quiz. It was good fun and a nice change to be staying in a place that had a bit of history as opposed to the identikit budget places made notorious by cheesy TV adverts.

A touch of flu hit the quiz master in early February but there was no rest for the sick. A trip to the north once more for a hotel quiz for a client who specialised in refridgeration. The guests proved to be chilled out. It was time to leave the mainland a week later with a flight to the Channel Islands.

The quiz was for a financial services company who invited various clients to a big hotel in the capital. The quiz had been running for several years before askTony were asked to get involved. Tradition dictated that before the quiz the guests were treated to an hour of live bingo from an elderly gentleman called John. Trying to start a lively quiz after the audience had been sent into a soporific slumber by a long wait waiting for clickety-click sixty six was a struggle. A swift pace was also not possible as the team with the organiser were always about ten minutes behind the other thirty teams, which meant questions had to be endlessly repeated.

The next quiz closer to home not far from Kings Cross featured an embarrassing cock-up just after the second question of the voices round. As the distinct tones of Keith Chegwin filled the venue, several voices shouted out "You did this round last year". I carried on regardless and checked the records at half time.

Notes on each quiz were recorded in an online database that was written by a Russian programmer I found on Scriptlance. So in theory mistakes like this should not have happened. Sometimes I got lazy and just wrote in "voices" in the review, rather than the actual voices that had been asked.

Later in February it was another local quiz, this time in Hemel Hempstead. It looked to be a straightforward event until the organiser told me just before kickoff that the winning team would receive £1,000 cash. Usually quiz nights only had token prizes, which afforded me some leeway with the marking, as nobody was taking it that seriously. But when big cash was up for grabs, the scores had to be perfect.

The month ended in Docklands with a quiz for a public sector regulator. The equipment got stuck in traffic in a taxi on the way to the venue so there was not much profit. There was no sign of the pace dropping though as bookings for March and April were literally flooding in.

The first March outing was an unusual booking – a Sunday lunchtime quiz for a couple's anniversary in a hotel not far from Stansted. The guests were an absolute delight and the event went so well I was buzzing for the next four days.

The euphoria lasted until I had to visit Bristol on the Thursday. Having navigated the congested M4, there was massive trouble trying to park. The quiz was taking place near the docks area. The venue proved a nightmare – full of pillars, and no DVD facility to play any video rounds. The audience were bad tempered and miserable, and the drive home took ages. I resolved never again to visit Bristol and it is a pledge that has stood the test of time.

I had two bookings the following week on the same night so tried a new strategy. I gave the first booking to my Dad as it was a regular client and he was keen to help out. We did a rehearsal the day before and I gave him several days to familiarise himself with the questions and the format. I went up to Solihull the same night my Dad was quiz mastering in the City of London, to do an event for a well-known electricity company. Client feedback on both events was excellent, although it remains the only quiz my Dad hosted as Mum said he did find it a bit stressful.

There was no time to relax after Solihull as the very next day I was off to Lancashire for a quiz in a cricket club near Rochdale. Only 5 teams turned up and the event was memorable because on arrival I was told the buffet being served halfway through would feature potato pie. I queried this with the chef to find out whether meat would also feature, only to be told there was no meat. It was a pastry pie with potato as the only ingredient. It did not prove popular and I had to content myself with a big Whopper meal from Burger King on the long drive home.

Three London events followed the week after, before it was time for another big trip north to Sunderland, one of the longest drives I ever did for a quiz night. The TV themes round was particularly popular featuring Dempsey and Makepeace, and Taggart, as well as the more recent tones of Strictly Come Dancing.

Due to Easter, I was able to take a break for a couple of weeks before resuming quiz action with a legal firm in the city of London. I was surprised to find an old university friend right in the middle of the audience, although given he studied law at college perhaps his presence was not all that unexpected. The quiz took place in an upmarket restaurant although the company subsequently received a life ban. The winners were given champagne and, overcome with the tremendous excitement of lifting the trophy, proceeded to shake it up and down like grand prix winners. They absolutely drenched the place including some expensive paintings and carpeting.

The day after it was another long drive this time with Mrs Roy as we travelled to Middlesbrough for a quiz for an ethical public sector body at the famous football stadium. This was a big event with well over 200 people sat for a big dinner followed by a quick-fire quiz. There was panic before the meal began when the organiser started worrying that the wine had not been ethically sourced, but a few glasses quickly placated her nerves. I was only on stage for about 45 minutes or so as the dinner had run over. Again, the most memorable aspect was not so much the quiz itself but the pre-match meal where we had relocated to a pub a mile or so round the corner. I ordered shepherd's pie and received the biggest plate of food I had seen in my life, absolutely dripping in gravy. It was closer to a soup than a pie but at the sum of £3.10 it was great value although sadly completely inedible.

A week later, after a quiz at a very swanky Surrey hotel, I was on the M5 down to Exeter for a pub event for an energy firm. I had booked a room at a nearby hotel to stay overnight, and having arrived in early afternoon, I was able to detour to Tavistock to visit my grandmother. It was to be my last visit to Devon as she moved into a nursing home in Bedfordshire a few months later.

There was still time in April for a big quiz in Kings College London for a legal firm, and a lively event for a consultancy at Walkabout on the Embankment. Of all the pub venues I had worked at, Walkabout always stands out due to the combination of its Australian clientele, striking décor, and smell of stale beer and vomit.

In May 2007 the first event for a television production company featured each team wearing different hats. Not sure why as it was not Halloween. I moved over to Elstree for the next quiz which was round the corner from where Big Brother is filmed. One of my favourite venues came next – a legal outfit just round the corner from Tower Bridge with spectacular views of the iconic landmark from the eight floor. The month finished with a trip to the scene of one of the best sporting moments from my childhood, albeit witnessed only via television. 1981 had seen the legend that is Ian Botham smash through the Australians at cricket grounds around the country. None more famous than the game where he scored 149 not out in the 3rd Test. Headingley Stadium in Leeds had executive suites overlooking the cricket ground and it was here I entertained (in the loosest sense of the word) a bingo company where the host complained there was absolutely no skill involved in the price is right round. Somebody should try telling that to Leslie Crowther.

There was controversy in early June when, at another event near Tower Bridge, the best feature of the quiz, the pizzas cooked in the venue's own pizza ovens, were served ridiculously slowly. There was such a delay I was forced to cancel the half-time break in the quiz when the pizzas were meant to be served, and just continued the questions. As a result, the quiz had actually finished by the time the mozzarella had sufficiently melted for the chef to deem them fit to serve

It was time for a brand new round later that month as

askTony gave a debut to a smells round which consisted of 10 test tubes rammed with cotton wool each infused with a particular fragrance. It was reasonably successful. There was a suggestion from the audience that next time I could feature a part of the body round which was duly noted and subsequently ignored.

A long drive to the south coast saw a visit to Poole in Dorset for a big consultancy firm. Notable was the first prize consisting of a £300 television for each contestant. It was a strange prize and took up a lot of room. My car miles were escalating sharply with a visit to Kent for an event at an incredibly tatty pub outside Rochester. The guests had been on an all-day bender so arrived paralytic. I cut the quiz from eight rounds to six and was back on the Dartford Crossing well ahead of time.

As the summer arrived, early July saw a lifetime opportunity to carry out a quiz at the theatre of dreams - Old Trafford in Manchester. I was surprised to be able to drive right under the South Stand, load the PA system into the lift, and arrive right in the heart of the stadium in the Stretford Suite. Next door the club had the Premier League trophy on display. It was a great night with an enthusiastic audience inspired by the view at such an historic sporting venue.

The next event was also very enjoyable for a firm that featured 28 guests, all of them Dutch. I had had to write a special set of questions as the usual Noel Edmonds type stuff would have gone down like a lead balloon. Before the quiz, the hosts had kindly treated me to a full 3 course meal – the same as enjoyed by the guests – and a bottle of wine. I remember next to nothing of the actual quiz.

In London a week later, there was a big quiz for a network of librarians who had surprisingly chosen a venue that was known as a very lively nightspot. The librarians lasted longer than the venue as it turned out as the latter was shut down a few months later following a fatal shooting.

At a quiz for a big airline a couple of days after, askTony

history was made with probably the most sought after prize we had featured. The client had generously provided each member of the winning team with a pair of return flights anywhere in the world. I had to be unusually scrupulous with the marking.

There was still time in July for a visit to the home of racing in Newmarket for an accountancy firm, although August was quiet with four London events for various firms. Although the petrol tank remained full, the bookings manager was racking up confirmations for the autumn period which meant once again all askTony records were going to be broken.

Eight events in September started with a trip to a minor university and the green Fens of Cambridge. It was an incredibly difficult venue to park anywhere near given the frankly ridiculous nature of the one-way system. Where you could drive, you struggled to get past the myriad of cyclists intent on owning the roads. Coupled with the ponderous tourists examining every sight, it remained one of my least favourite quiz locations for a number of years.

Next up was another day with two events the same night. So whilst Gary entertained a law firm on the banks of the Thames, I was up in Bradford in a well-known hotel chain performing for some chemical people. Or pharmacists as they are better known. The roast beef sandwiches were particularly good, but Bradford was a long drive – three and a half hours to get there, slightly less coming back.

Just as I was recovering from that drive, it was time to go to the depths of the New Forest for another hotel event for a managed services company quite well known for dealing with prisons. It was a struggle to get any food for the quizmaster, but the evening went down well. It was well after ten when the quiz started as they were having a big meal beforehand, so it was the very early hours before vehicle and driver made it back to base.

Having negotiated Bradford in the north, and Hampshire

in the south, it was time to stretch the points of the compass with a visit to Cheltenham in the west. It is a town not greatly blessed with good access roads as I had known to my cost during school days when we frequently had to drive there cross country from Bedford. So despite only being seventy miles from home, it was a tortuous two hours trek to find the venue. Feedback from the client afterwards was excellent as apparently previous quiz masters had just sat at the front and read out questions, so they were not used to a compere walking round the room doing some interactions with the audience.

The only part of the country I had not visited in the month was the east, so it made sense the next trip was to Essex to the county town of Chelmsford. Known for their love of drinking and clubbing, I expected it to be a lively night and they did not disappoint.

After so much travelling it was a relief that September closed with two London events. The second, for a tax outfit, featured by special client request a round about the tax outfit with ten questions written by the organiser. That round went down as well as a Health Secretary addressing the nursing union, although the rest of the quiz was well received. If you are going to insist on having a company round, the trick is to make it something funny or interesting about the employees like what they looked like as children, or guess the first record they bought, rather than the taxable profit the Bromley branch made last year.

As the nights drew colder, October started with one of my regular events for the sports club in London. The second event of the month featured another venue that had been known for various nightclubs right in the heart of London. After the quiz, bad times returned as it folded a few months later. One of the rounds involved identifying some famous faces from just their eyes. It proved too hard for the audience and was never seen again.

After a third quiz in October where the guests arrived

drunk and got even further inebriated as the questions wore on, I made it to Victoria for a quiz for an estate agency. Not for the first time the food proved the main talking point. It never ceased to amaze me that a venue would be happy to take hundreds of pounds from a client and their sixty guests, but do the absolute minimum in terms of catering, and sometimes even below that. On this occasion stale sandwiches that were curling at the sides were all that was on offer to refresh the participants.

Another quality venue followed down by the Thames where the main discovery was that bottles of chilled Corona with lime goes down the quizmaster's throat very nicely. It was time to visit the wonders of Milton Keynes next for an insurance company, and then straight back to London the following night for an event at a pub in Docklands.

An interesting day the week after when I attempted two quiz nights on the same day with a very tight timescale. First off to Slough for a chocolate bar manufacturer. It was a two-hour quiz slot in early afternoon, and I had to dip into several reserve rounds to fill the whole time slot. As soon as the event was over, I was off to the city of London for a law firm. Slough to the city took about ninety minutes as it was rush hour. A very tired quizmaster arrived back home around midnight with a dry throat from all the questions asked.

Nothing against Guildford but it is a real pain to get to unless you happen to live on that south western side of greater London. Ordinarily if a quiz enquiry came in from that region, the bookings manager was under instructions to double the price to counter the inconvenience, but on this occasion the gig slipped through the net. It is another town like Cambridge besieged by a complicated one-way system, so it was a relief the car made it there and back in one piece. The timings I had been given for the quiz were completely out, and at the time when the guests had supposedly finished eating and the quiz was due to start, they were in fact still on their poppadum starters.

The month closed in Lambeth in London for a banking firm who provided excellent food. However, their two TVs did not have VGA sockets, so video rounds were problematic.

There was no time to reflect on just how much quiz business was booming as November opened on the first day with a visit to what used to be one of London's tallest buildings – Centrepoint in Tottenham Court Road. This tower block has one of the world's most unforgiving car parks with sheer concrete posts and a design for parking spaces modelled on Legoland rather than the real world. If you make it into the car park in one piece, it is another massive battle to get through security and into the building. The lifts do not have any buttons so where you end up is conditional on what has pressed on the ground floor reception. Battle three is to persuade security to part with one of their packing trolleys to use for the speakers and laptop. Once negotiated, the view from the upper floors is rather good unless you are unfortunate to have a cloudy day, or as on this occasion, darkness has fallen as it was after five o-clock.

After a venue like Centrepoint, it was a relief for traditional pub event next up with parking right outside, albeit at exorbitant London rates. The pub itself sold an interesting range of lagers none of which was drinkable, but as I was driving the opportunity did not arise in any case. As a quiz venue, it was not ideal as it featured many nooks and corners so most of the teams could not see each other. There were also a number of pillars so any video rounds were impossible.

The theme for the month was challenging venues as number three in November was a restaurant in central London next to a theatre. I had been warned the venue was small, but I was not expecting to set up in a space about the size of a bathroom sink. In the end the only way I could wire everything up was to open the door of the disabled toilet I was next to and balance the speakers on a spare chair wedging the door open.

As punishment for booking three difficult venues in a row,

it was time for Mrs Roy to carry out a quiz and so she set off by train for Sunderland. We had established the venue had a built-in PA system so she didn't need to take one. The guests absolutely loved her, and Karen was pleased to have a break from looking after our two young children, if only for one night. My next event was another outing to south London for the Conservative club followed by a first ever trip to Dorking for a big pharmaceutical. The hotel was a lovely place but had an unusual sound policy where, if you used their PA system but went over a certain volume, the sound would cut out. This caused me considerable irritation, but it did not actually affect the event that much.

There followed three events in central London which all went pretty much to plan before a trip to the exclusive Champneys resort near Portsmouth. Arriving in the early evening in the dark, it was quite a weird place as there was absolutely nobody about. Presumably all the guests were soaking somewhere private, but it was a struggle to find anyone to tell me which room to set up in.

A twelve-event month concluded with a return to Tower Bridge to find the pizza pub had fixed their timing issues, and a few stops further down the Docklands Light Railway, a pre-Christmas event for an accountancy outfit at a Hilton hotel.

December started with a trip to Windsor to see the Queen. She was not in, so I ended up at a restaurant near a bridge. It was a good group and a classy venue, although the client had insisted on twenty company questions which was about nineteen too many.

A law firm in London and a return trip to Cheltenham were followed by another visit to the Guildford area for an animal charity. This was their big Christmas event, and the drink and food made for a great atmosphere. At the end of the quiz I was unusually requested to stay on and act as a DJ, which given my music tastes was always a risk. After a couple of songs they all enjoyed, I managed to clear the dance floor with something far too slow before rescuing things quickly with Dancing Queen.

A rare Sunday event – only the second ever – followed in Essex and being a family occasion, it was a nice mix of guests and nothing too strenuous in terms of questions. There were three Christmas events in the following week all in Central London, and then a surprise return to Windsor (given I had not visited in the previous five years). All of this served as a warm-up for the busiest day in askTony history so far.

On Friday 12th December 2007 we broke new ground for askTony quiz nights. Three events in one day. The plan was for me to carry out the first which was starting about 11am near Liverpool Street in London. Then Karen would be running a lunchtime event just off the Strand, before I was off to east London for an afternoon Christmas party. The advantage in the planning stage was that hopefully we would all be home to put our feet up for a relaxing Friday evening.

There was a fly in the ointment, or more specifically, swollen nodules in the throat as the day dawned with the quizmaster having lost his voice. Luckily, there was no illness to accompany it, but the first quiz did have a host doing his best impression of the legendary snooker commentator, whispering Ted Lowe.

A quick drive over to the Strand saw me touch base with Karen and there was immediate disappointment when it turned out the pub the quiz was taking place in had a television apparently ten years old with no inputs other than a terrestrial aerial. So we had to reluctantly abandon the video round as there was nothing to plug into. Karen soldiered on and reported later the quiz passed off quietly but without apparent incident.

With a throat as dry as sandpaper, I headed over to the Wanstead area to meet a group who had clearly and rightly been drinking all day as it was their Christmas party. It was a colourful quiz as I remember hats being worn but in truth I could have been hallucinating.

The year finished with a double event on the same day the

following week. I had a short trip to Battersea, whereas Karen was reconnecting with her northern routes with a return trip to Sheffield. Both events passed off successfully and we collapsed in exhaustion after an incredibly busy year.

Our turkey preparations were not in any way interrupted when we received a churlish complaint letter regarding the Strand event from the finance manager of the client company.

> We had our company Christmas party last Friday and your company was booked to provide the quiz. It was enjoyed by most people but I am disappointed that the high cost was not reflective of the quality of the quiz provided.

> Essentially it was in the format of a pub quiz and quite frankly, we could have taken the questions off any number of websites. It was certainly not "individually prepared to take account of the profile of the audience" as stated on your website and certainly the promoted use of the "latest technology such as computerised scoring, video questions, all running off high spec laptop computers" did not materialise. I understand there was a problem with the pubs video system, but surely you should have done a recce of the site before hand and should be inclusive of the fee.

> I honestly feel that although the evening was fun, it was not value for money. I hope that given this feedback and that we didn't get the "true experience" you will consider crediting us for some of the cost.

There was no basis for this complaint as nobody said anything at the time of the quiz. It looked like a desperate and unnecessary attempt to claw some money back for Christmas. We didn't lose any sleep over this, although statistically it did take Karen's complaint ratio up whilst mine remained at zero.

Photo 9 Conference quiz celebrations in July 2007

Photo 10 Christmas in Wanstead in December 2007

Photo 11 A proud moment as my Dad makes his quiz hosting debut in 2007

8 UNIVERSALLY CHALLENGED

A pattern that emerged in 2007 continued as we hit January in the new year. For every quiz booked, there was a trail of enquiries that just went cold. A long runner over several weeks had been a lady called Gosia who had originally booked a quiz for November 28th. After several conversations, it was eventually postponed until early January. Then on final confirmation, it turned out the whole event was cancelled as their Chief Executive had resigned.

It was a similar story from Kate who worked for a well know client services company. It all looked on, until an email on the 10th January informing us that they had decided to do something different this time.

We were also beginning to discover the amazing differences between clients in how much preparation they put in to choosing and booking a quiz night. January 2008 saw a lot of conversation with a leading building society who were looking for an annual quiz night for all national finance journalists to be held at the end of February. They were, the email said, contemplating whether to get the questions outsourced.

The email went on to specify the five rounds they would like, which were to consist of Sport, Fine Wine, News, Music, and a Picture Round. They also wanted an interactive round called wine tasting. Karen and I had a conversation about it and decided this client was going to take a lot of our energy, so we agreed to let it go. Hopefully, the evening was a massive drunken success with plenty of wine drunk interactively.

We tended to get a lot of enquiries from charities, such as this one from a well-known hospice. The client specified that because of the people that will be attending, the questions were going to have to be more "highbrow" than the other pub quizzes the correspondent had attended in the past. But she was keen to point out she was not looking for a snobby vibe, but the whole theme of the evening was going to be refined entertainment.

This sort of specification again set alarm bells ringing with me, as it sounded like the organiser wanted to vet the questions. This was something we almost never allowed. Interestingly the client specified that one table at the event would be made up of newsreaders including Natasha Kaplinsky. The other nine tables would comprise city bosses. With a polite, thanks but no thanks, we decided not to offer our services.

There was plenty of real quiz action and some travel to occupy askTony. In February it was off to an exclusive hotel a few miles outside Edinburgh for a bank quiz that only lasted one hour after dinner. It was a long way to travel, but sufficiently lucrative to make it worthwhile. A week later, it was a visit to a conference centre just outside Derby. Again, it was only for a 60-minute quiz taking place for 130 delegates who were sat at tables of ten.

Another trip to the Channel Islands followed, where I made the mistake of starting the quiz right under one of the venues speakers resulting in some ear-splitting feedback that caused a couple of elderly guests to have minor heart attacks. A busy month ended in the splendour of the Birmingham Metropole for another banking outfit. As well as quizmaster, I had been asked to be the compere linking the whole evening. The agenda had been sent to me a few days before:

7.30 p.m. Dinner call

7.40 p.m. Introduction to the evening

7.45 p.m. Grace followed by First course

8.00 p.m. Round 1 - In the News

8.15 p.m. Second course

8.30 p.m. Round 2 - Movie Clips video

8.45 p.m. Main Course

9.10 p.m. Round 3 - Sports Action video

9.25 p.m. Dessert

9.40 p.m. Round 4 - Pop Music

9.55 p.m. Cheeseboard

10.05 p.m. Speeches

10.15 p.m. Comfort break

10.30 p.m. Dancing

Results of the Quiz to be announced when the Band take a break (approx. 11.30).

I did manage to get the results moved to take place during the comfort break as there was no way I was hanging around the bowels of the Birmingham Metropole until 11.30. The main challenge such an agenda posed was, in my experience, there was no way any catering outfit at these hotels would stick to the published schedule. Credit to the hotel though – on this occasion they managed it, and everybody left happy.

A couple of nights later, I was in central London for a food quiz for a legal company who had their own in-house chef. We had already had a few conversations prior to the event and had come up with a format to create a special culinary trivia event as follows. There were 5 mystery food objects, including an unusual vegetable, and a unique cooking utensil; there were 10 songs, all with a type of fruit in the title. An ingredients round followed, together with the price is right. We had taken the tasting menus from a few London restaurants, and the contestants had to guess the price. The quiz concluded with a name the chef picture round.

It was back to Centrepoint in early March for another battle with the car park, and a particularly unforgiving milk trolley which was employed to wheel the speakers into position. I stayed in London for several other events that month including a quiz for a mobile tech company. What was interesting from talking to their representative was they had a £3,000 budget every two months for staff events. Given how much we charged, they must have had a lot of money left to stick behind the bar.

The two big events that required fresh questions and a lot of preparation had been the Centrepoint event and the food quiz. But the advantage of this was it allowed me to re-use a few of the rounds at the other events.

A favourite question in the news round was question 10 which was always a birthday-based age question based on celebrities. Typically, the format was:

> Put these 4 in order of age starting with the youngest:
>
> the actor Kevin Costner
>
> the musician Jools Holland
>
> the football manager Jose Mourinho
>
> the snooker player Dennis Taylor

This question always generated a discussion within a team and could be made harder or easier with a relatively simple tweak. I had also become attached to a round called Think of a Number, where teams had white boards and had to write a figure down based on a random fact. They held up the boards and the team that was nearest got the points. This round usually started by asking contestants how many toilets were at the newly opened Wembley Stadium. Over 2,000 is the answer.

April saw another bunch of enquiries that led nowhere. The first was for the wealth division of a major bank who wanted one hour in Glasgow. Given the travel involved, we quoted the most expensive fee ever for a quiz and were not surprised when the bank decided to use somebody they had worked with before. We also had a call from The Ritz hotel who wanted a quiz for 50-70 staff who worked there. They had been quoted £400 by a competitor but said that fee was far too high. We decided not to quote. Another lady who had been at the film quiz wanted to know if we also ran Bingo evenings. We said no. A firm who had booked last year were contacted to see if they wanted to repeat the fun. The answer was negative. This year they were going to the snow dome instead. A firm of architects in Tower Bridge wanted a quiz. It all looked positive until Karen rang them back to confirm and discovered a local pub had offered to provide the quiz for £100.

There was plenty of opportunity to get out and about, starting with an event fairly near Silverstone, where once again Think of A Number made an appearance. It took place at a hotel and was another after dinner quiz so there was a fair amount of waiting in the bar before I was eventually called to perform.

At the regular quiz for the sports club in West London, I attempted a new round using mobile phones. It was billed as Tony's Text a Tenner and consisted of reading out a question and letting anybody in the audience text in their answer. It worked reasonably well but was not very visual so it didn't make a re-appearance. There were also events for an IT firm in Berkhamsted and a financial firm in the West End. The latter event was in a pub full of pillars, so no video was possible.

The audience was also very international, and the sports round focused probably too much on UK sport so feedback was duly noted.

May was an enjoyable month hosting, starting with a legal firm by the Thames. I then literally moved about five hundred metres the following night at a pub in St Katherine's Dock. It was closer to home the next week with a quiz near Hemel Hempstead for a media firm who offered a prize for the winning team of £400. This was unusually generous although highly unoriginal prize, and was largely due to the social committee having a big underspend. There was also an opportunity to send Karen on her annual trip to Sunderland; another event that went down very well.

We took tentative requests from a firm in Chessington who wanted a pop quiz at the end of their biannual meeting which would also feature a barbecue. We said no. There was a call from a firm in Chichester which was on a Saturday night, so although we were close to confirming, in the end we decided it would take up a lot of the weekend. A firm in Weston Super Mare were having a corporate team building event at a pub that would include skittles, darts and pool. They thought a quiz would add an extra dimension and they were probably right. But it all sounded a bit low budget and the prospect of a first ever visit to Weston did not appeal.

June started with another daunting audience of head teachers in the Midlands. Given the discipline these professionals would be used to dishing out in their day jobs, you would expect a competitive but fair quiz. Not a bit of it. Of all the events I have carried out, this featured the most cheating and bickering, and extensive use of google via various devices. A week later in the city, a famous bank broke the drinking record for an askTony quiz with a bar bill extending into the high thousands.

The events that never materialised included an approach from Suzie who wanted a dinner quiz somewhere near Junction 14 of the M40. She wanted six rounds but was insist-ent one of these should be about logistics relating to her company. A firm in Dorset wanted a quiz to follow a family barbecue but only needed sixty minutes. Given several nightmare experiences of driving to Dorset for family events, and the lack of any viable motorways in the region, that was a firm no. A golf club in Essex had a client who spent weeks haggling on price and then decided to book with somebody else. A notorious bank was interested in running a series of quiz nights at universities across the UK. It looked big budget project, and a serious proposal, so I duly travelled to their Liverpool Street offices with a slide deck and pitch. I was met by a committee of 12 people who seemed to be working on the project full-time. The chief organiser seemed happy with our proposal but then disappeared into radio silence in the weeks after.

In July I started the month in an unusual venue at the Boat House in Hyde Park. I was worried about parking arrangements, but it did not prove to be a problem. There was a 30th birthday quiz in the city that went very well, with some questions tailored to celebrating thirty years. An event the following week took place at a nightclub in the centre of town. It was a big audience of over one hundred, and there was a technical problem with the back speakers. Unfortunately two teams sat by them and could not hear the quiz, although as I was based in the centre of the venue with the other sixteen teams, I wasn't aware of this. Staying in London just up from Oxford Circus we did a quiz featuring some fun facts about the guests, all of these were supplied by the client pre-event:

> I had to babysit the cheeky girls for a whole evening a couple of years ago (In their pre-MP shagging days).

> I was once caught on the sofa at 9am on New Years Day asleep in the arms of Mrs X by Mr X whilst stay-

ing at their house over New Years.

I once manhandled Yoko Ono outside Ronnie Scotts in Soho.

I once gave a famous premier league football manager a lift home in my car from a party

I did the voice over for a TV ad that appeared in England vs Argentina in the world cup.

I was the British Hang Gliding Champion

I played the Angel Gabriel in their school nativity not once but twice during their school career

I'm afraid of the number 3

I once went skinny-dipping in a lake at a work conference

That format had worked well at some previous events and could either be used in a single multiple-choice round (depending on how well the audience knew each other) or as a bonus question in between rounds. At an event for a services company the following night, I received another very specific agenda that included a mouth-watering list of canapes:

Lavender & honey-glazed baby Cumberland sausages

Cajun spiced chicken kebab with a lemon & lime cream

Chargrilled chorizo & roasted pepper

Cajun king prawn brochette tossed in lemon & garlic butter

Crab, green onion & coriander cake, peppered sour cream

Mini Yorkshire puddings, caramelised shallots, chives & Brie

Roasted tomato, artichoke & pine nut crostini with balsamic glaze

Tempura of bell peppers with a soft herb mayonnaise

Unfortunately, and not for the first time, the quiz master had been left out of the catering, so I had to watch forlornly as the guests tucked in.

A lady who worked for a leisure firm was in touch. She informed us she was looking for a professionally produced quiz perhaps with electronic answer devices and something a little bit different from the norm. She had a celebrity in attendance, and it may be that she wanted them to deliver the quiz. We replied, and never heard from her again.

A firm in Surrey were having a team briefing at a local pub and wanted the quiz to start straight after the talk at 2pm. It did not sound as though the team briefing was going to give good news, so we turned it down. An NHS trust were looking for a quiz for 100 people in Kent. We agreed a fee and a lot of specific details but then were called to be told the chair had decided not to go ahead.

A lady called Joy who worked for a wealth management firm wanted a quiz in East London but said askTony was too expensive. Keeley called asking for a quiz in Bolton; we rang her back the following week to discover she had been sacked. Samantha wanted a pub quiz host with fun and innovative questions who would encourage banter between the teams but not be too cheeky. We called her and said that would be a problem as our quiz host specialised in asking dull and boring questions, and his style was to get the audience to remain in complete silence and hostility.

August arrived, and the first quiz of the month required me to arrive perfectly sober and driving within the speed limit. It took place at the headquarters of a north west policing centre. The audience proved surprisingly literary, and excellent at the famous opening lines of novels round. A couple of days later it was time to visit the home of horse racing in Newmarket for an accountancy firm. The winning team was called Septimus Maximus and it turned out they had won the quiz every year since records began. Following the trip to racing headquarters, it was next over to the home of tennis at Wimbledon, and an event just outside number one court. No photos were allowed as the audience consisted of future tennis champions who were at some sort of two-week summer school.

A lady called Juanita was in contact about an event at Christmas for an Oxford academic institution. We agreed a price but then the Dean apparently blocked the go-ahead. AOL got in touch, but their scheduled event was called off when the company suffered a merger. Accenture were contacted to see if they wanted to book again but they had decided to have a night at the dogs instead. And an insurance firm wanted an event in October at Kingston Working Men's Club, but after a quote, we never heard from them again.

September and October 2008 saw 11 quiz nights mainly taking place in the London area. There was a trip to Milton Keynes for an insurance firm. I attempted to run a buzzer round in West London but the buzzers proved decided wobbly on the technology side, so I stuck with a previous decision not to employ them in the majority of the quiz nights.

Karen spent a lot of time chasing people who had booked in previous years, but there were also some notable new enquiries. The Kuwaiti Investment Centre got in touch apparently keen on a quiz, but when we rang back for confirmation, we were told the staff had voted on a number of activities and the quiz had come bottom of the staff vote. A pharmaceutical company were enthusiastic about the prospect of a quiz in Brighton. They then had second thoughts and decided to invest in a Wii console and spend the day playing interactive games.

In November I carried out a quiz for an insurance firm in the City in a venue I had used before. This time I managed for the first time to connect into the pub's sound system which involved plugging an XLR jack into the wall. Unfortunately, they did not have any speakers by the door, so again the teams sat in that vicinity were in trouble. Two nights later there was a different technical challenge in Beckenham when the in-house system had packed up the previous day. I used my two speakers which, due to the limit of cable length, only stretched halfway down the massive room. People at the back complained they could not hear.

The following week on Remembrance Day I travelled to Solihull for a return booking that had been confirmed months before. I arrived at the venue to find the manager all prepared with food ready and bar stocked. Ten minutes past the agreed start time we were both alarmed to see the venue still empty and no sign of any guests. A call was placed to the organiser who revealed he had thought the quiz was the following night. A check of all the paperwork revealed him to be wrong, so I packed up and travelled the hundred miles back home with another first in askTony history. A quiz fixture abandoned without a question being asked. Incidentally, the venue was not free the following evening and nor was I, so there was to be no re-arrangement and no refund of the fee charged.

In the final month of the year I went over to Cheltenham for a housing company, and then to Windsor for a repeat of the previous year's quiz. I visited a South Irish Club to do a quiz for a well-known Trades Union, and finished the year in Sheffield, another repeat booking, with a record 24 teams taking part.

2008 showed the first decline in annual bookings for ask-Tony having peaked in 2007, but it was still a remarkably busy year. Overall askTony had now completed 444 quiz nights.

Photo 12 Champagne celebrations in the Midlands in 2008

9 TEQUILA MOCKINGBIRD

Another new year and time in the first event of 2009 to give a debut to a new round format called General Knowledge Knockout. This was a reworked version of millionaire, with the questions getting gradually harder. If you got one wrong or left one blank, you were knocked out. The safety conscious could of course stick, and hand in prior to answering the next question. There were a few variations on this format. You could ask the teams who wanted to hand in, prior to asking the next question. Or you could ask who wanted to hand in after asking the question. Either way the round worked well and was added to my retained list.

It was a trip up the A5 next to Hinckley, a football club famous for giving Luton, Burnley, Brentford and Watford the pacey striker Andre Gray. A quick google reveals the venue has now been taken over by Jury's Inn. On arrival in the Black Picasso, I realised I had visited the venue before as it had a curious moat/river in front of it in a bizarre attempt to give the illusion of class.

February saw two clients who had booked before. First, a trip to Birmingham for the meticulously organised dinner quiz. 24 hours later, I was in the maternity ward of the Luton & Dunstable hospital where Karen gave birth to our 3rd child Lily. They were in hospital for a few days, so on Tuesday a visit from the northern grandparents allowed me to take a short flight to the Channel Islands for some more pre-quiz bingo before 35 teams got down to some serious quiz action.

There was a slight problem back in London the next week when the promised buffet was not delivered to the tables during half time. And another new round was unveiled – on this day in previous years. This round was relatively easy to research and compile, and gave the quiz a personal touch as if the event was scheduled for 10th March – the 10 questions would be about events that happened on the 10th March in previous years. I could throw in some history, a bit of sport, general knowledge, a video question, a touch of music – it was quiz gold.

We did have a couple of events cancelled in February and March which was unusual but not too surprising looking back given the economic times. The energy supplier struggled for numbers for their quiz, and an accountancy firm who usually spared no expense could not justify the fee this time.

A lucrative event was declined as too near Lily's due date. English speaking attendees from Europe, the Middle East and India had been promised. It would not have been a great advert for gender equality though as 90% of the attendees would have been male. A 3-hour minimum trip to Dorset would not have added to the fun.

A man called David had spent several months arranging a quiz in the Earls Court area of London on behalf of a mystery client who may well have made boilers. It got all the way to the invoicing stage until the week before when the mystery client cancelled, presumably due to a pilot light going out somewhere.

A clear sign the economy was on the downturn was provided by Maria who worked for a financial firm near Liverpool Street. She secured a venue called The Poet (which did not last long) but a couple of weeks before the event an apology email came through. Her division was undergoing lots of changes. Her original director would probably not be in place. Her new boss looked after many more projects across Europe, The Far East, and America. He had reviewed priorities and decided a trivia night was not a good use of budget.

The client who had booked the big Oscars night the previous year assured us all through December, January, and February that the event was going ahead in early March. We invoiced in late January. Our contact disappeared to Switzerland and our new representative rang to cancel a week before. She was unfortunately the victim of a change to our terms and conditions so for the first time we were able to charge a cancellation fee.

Luckily, an international bank had no such trouble in late March and the drinks flowed throughout the evening. With the handheld microphone, I spent a lot of the quiz moving between the tables and noticed a lot of mobile phone usage going on. The prizes were insignificant and the venue reception pretty poor, so it was not a big problem – this was a few years before Wi-Fi in pubs/restaurants became taken for granted. The burgers that were served tasted superb, but the quiz master must have had a dodgy one because several hours later there were unfortunate repercussions.

As a result, the event the following evening had to be cancelled which was the first time ever I had had to cry off due to sickness.

There was an event the following night and there was no way I was going to miss two in a row so a slightly pasty individual turned up just round the corner from Tower Bridge to deliver questions for 150. Five days later a very convenient location saw a quiz delivered for the first time ever at a motorway service station.

The venue was a few miles from the start of the M1 and the client one of the big names in service stations. It was a good group who embraced the karaoke and as they were all staying on site, they drank the bar dry. Sadly, I couldn't join in as the motor was waiting to take me back to London Luton.

It was back to Centrepoint at the start of April for another very alcoholic quiz which included a round where the guests had to identify several different drinks. Each had been poured out into hundreds of small containers. The room the round was set in was sealed and, being several hundred feet in the sky, had no openable windows. It was no surprise that just walking into the room was intoxicating.

In London the same month we had a video round called That was the Year which included a series of events culled from youTube and the teams just had to guess the year each event happened. It proved popular and was used again.

The final event in April took place just off a square in Holborn, in central London. It was held in the basement of a pub which had a few pillars, no sound system and no built in TVs. It was all a bit of an effort to install my stuff; the projector was perched precariously on a bar stool, the screen set at a slight angle. Despite the difficulties, the quiz went down well and ended in a tiebreak settled by an Olympics question.

askTony took in only its second ever trip to Exeter the following week and it proved expensive. Attempting to negotiate a needlessly complicated one-way system, I ended up a few minutes away from the venue in a multi-storey car park. The long drive had taken its toll and a slight miscalculation turning on the 4th level resulted in a big scrape of the passenger door. Black car and white concrete pillar did not work well together. A claim on insurance for £910 was the result following the garage evaluation and repair.

May 2009 was proving busy and there was still time for quiz at the London headquarters of a international law firm, some questions at a tennis club in Berkhamsted, and the first of three events for the same television production company. The client in question had several shift and temporary workers and the only way to include them all was to stage several different quizzes over a number of weeks.

A couple of London events followed – the second close to Tower Bridge again, and this time I was able to make use of their in-house parking which made life a lot easier. Despite the prestigious offices, the sound system left a lot to be desired. If you stood with a microphone anywhere near the ceiling speakers, the feedback was screeching. And the installers had not been shy at putting in speakers. The result was like a disco hopscotch of trying to move around the audience whilst dodging the feedback areas.

At home with three children under five Karen was doing a brilliant job of manning the phones trying to get new business. One client we were chasing had a contact called Lynne. After a couple of calls with no answer, we got an email to say Lynne had retired and we should try Marcia. Marcia told us relatively quickly not to waste her time but to try Sue. Sue initially proved elusive but eventually revealed their social events were determined every year at a committee meeting that took place in January.

Sharon made us feel incredibly special. She had been in touch asking about a quiz for 120 people, a bit of music, a spot of buffet, what price could we do. We replied with a detailed quote but it turned out quiz came bottom of the staff poll when asked what night out they wanted.

The number of enquiries that were pursued vigorously and then nothing came of them had by mid-2009 probably exceeded 50. Very rarely was it the other way round, where Karen and I decided to pull out of an event. One such occasion followed a detailed phone conversation at the end of June where things were agreed, and emails exchanged. During many subsequent emails and telephone calls, it emerged the event was for an anniversary. The quiz was to take place following a big dinner. A magician was also going to feature. The quiz was not going to start until at least 10 possibly later. The venue was an absolute nightmare to work in. Part of the quiz needed to be hosted on a six-foot suspended stage. The couple wanted to vet the questions. The enquiry was taking up a considerable amount of energy and time.

With a week to go we reluctantly pulled out of the event with obviously no money exchanged. The client did not take the news at all well, calling it disgraceful in fact, but given we were not in the habit of doing this, and the quiz was not the centre piece of the evening, we were quite confident the evening would have passed off just as successfully without our involvement.

Whilst that enquiry was running its course, we did manage to squeeze in a few summer events. A London evening saw an audience of scriptwriters complain about the movie round as they wanted films which featured subtitles. A printing company made the unusual decision to restrict the number of people allowed in a team to just three. And a law enforcement agency north of Manchester struggled badly to identify celebrity faces in the photo round. A request was put in to replace with photos of football grounds for next year's event.

In early September I discovered it was relatively easy to park for free in the centre of Cambridge. Provided you knew the right hotel. I was quite proud of the rounds that featured in this quiz. We opened as usual with a news round. I always liked to start that round with a really big, significant and serious news question, and that night it was no different. Question one round one was:

> This week saw the retirement of one of the group Chas and Dave. Which member has left the band?

In the same round we learnt that Baroness Scotland was in trouble for employing an illegal immigrant, the Pope announced he was visiting Britain, and that Martina Hingis had been the first contestant to be voted off Strictly Come Dancing. Asked to put Declan Donnelly, Liam Gallagher and Catherine Zeta Jones in order of age starting with the youngest, most teams struggled. A selection of cities photos comprised round two. Come Dine with Me opened the TV themes third round. In round four guests had watched a series of archive clips and had to name the year the event took place. We saw action from the Poll Tax riots, Shane Warne bowling Mike Gatting with his first ball, and the first ever broadcast on Channel 4.

Famous Lines was the first round after the break for food,

including this gem:

> Once upon a time there were four little Rabbits, and their names were - Flopsy, Mopsy, Cotton-tail, and Peter.

In our movie clips round there were scenes from 12 Monkeys, 28 Days Later, and the Lion King amongst others. In the round before the big finish, punters had to write down the next line when the music stopped. We had performances from Gloria Gaynor, Elton John, and the Ting Tings interspersed with Jason Donovan, Robbie Williams, and Tiffany.

The finale was general knowledge knockout where the questions got progressively harder. The simpler opener was:

> Cider is a drink traditionally made from which fruit?

For 10 points, if teams were still going at question five, they could have attempted:

> The Persistence of Memory is a famous work by which famous painter?

And only the truly brave tackled the 60th and final question in the quiz:

> Greeks and Romans considered which herb to be a symbol of mortality?

The quizmaster had tucked in heartily to the buffet provided. This was in part relief at not having to read out a business round that the client had threatened to provide, and which traditionally proved neither entertaining, nor high scoring. In an unprecedented event that was never repeated, the six members of the winning team all had ginger hair.

It was time to visit the outskirts of Birmingham in early October not once, but twice in three days. It was a pair of events for a car dealership. Each event was to have 40 people, ages ranging from 20s to 50s. On both days, guests would be in training from 2.30pm and then settling down to a buffet with quiz in the evening. During the booking process the client had specifically vetoed the price is right round, as being car dealers, they were doing something similar in the scheduled training. It proved remarkably easy to park right outside the suite where the event took place, and both nights were received very well.

We were in Covent Garden later that month for an event for a respected newspaper group. Although the pub concerned occupied a prestigious spot, it proved remarkably badly equipped for audiovisual facilities. I had to drag all my stuff including projector, screen and PA system on a back-breaking slog from just south of Tottenham Court Road. The event was hosted by an old mate of mine from Redwood who was working at the newspaper. He had a background in advertising sales so proved remarkably adept behind the mike.

I was pleased to pick up another local booking before the month ended with a trip to Milton Keynes for an insurance company. It was a Saturday night and the client had booked a company to run a casino when the quiz ended. They needed me to stay on and provide background music until midnight. The quiz ran from 6-9, with the blackjack then taking over. The birthday question in round one again featured a cracking line-up, with the congregation asked to put Julia Roberts, Sinitta, and Danni Minogue in order of age starting with the youngest. It was also a night where a new round got its debut. Feeding off the enthusiasm for Countdown but having been stung by how the atmosphere could be killed with an anagrams round as everybody went silent trying to concentrate, Tony's word wheel was born.

Eight letters were arranged around a single central letter in a wheel. Teams had to make as many words as they could in a time limit. The audience were relatively engaged but it proved a bit of a pain to mark and brought insistences that words existed when they did not. So Tony's word wheel emulated the great Michael Ricketts who famously played just 45 minutes for England's football team in his career by only appearing once at a quiz night.

Once the quiz and the casino finished there was not a lot of people left so my DJ efforts went almost unnoticed.

It was off to the historic market town of Uxbridge five days later for an oil firm event. Looking through the TV round we had some absolute belters that night including the theme tune to Property Ladder, a show symptomatic of its time for people being desperate to get on the property ladder. However, the world was now recovering from the financial crisis, so the novelty of the show had worn off.

It is worth reflecting on that oil quiz as getting to and from the event was far more work that carrying out the quiz itself. Whenever I complained to myself about such matters, I quickly reflected that some people went down the mines for forty years; I was being asked to drive to a venue, carry some equipment, speak into a microphone, more often than not get free food and drink, and then drive home again.

On this occasion the instructions were as follows. The room the event was to be held in was a private room above the main restaurant. I was to park at the Chime shopping centre (note this is not free). There was no lift. The venue had no audio or video equipment. In some ways such clarity made things easier in that I knew I was using all my own stuff, and not reliant on venue equipment which often was pretty dodgy. With my visit to the Chime – now under new management – I knew what to expect.

The opening round – the news round – was a beast. The odious BNP leader had been on Question Time causing much controversy the previous week – all the punters had to do was name him (Nick Griffin). Formula 1 provided two points for question two if you could name where the final race of the World Championship was being staged in. Next up I played a clip of the classic track from Cheryl (in those days called

Cole) where she urged everyone to Fight For This Love. You just had to identify the singer and artist. It was topical because unbelievably it had just become the fastest selling song of 2009.

People tend to be money conscious particularly if they work, as this group did, for an oil company. Question four posed the conundrum how much a first class stamp cost as a postal strike was underway. The big political news of the week, for Luton at least, was that Esther Rantzen had declared herself as a candidate for Luton South in the 2010 General Election despite having zero interest in Luton and zero connections with the town. An old favourite when I was struggling for questions was to slip in some reference to the current Pope and ask what the roman numerals were after his name. In Benedict's case it was XVI. We kept it worldwide with a teaser about the name of the Afghan President forced into a re-run of the election. A man by the name of Hamid Karzai was the answer.

Looking back at these questions now, I realised every question in the opening news round referenced the same newspaper – and the reason for that of course was I had done a quiz for that newspaper the previous week. A tedious question about the world's longest golf course that had recently opened was number eight. Immediately followed by an old staple of the latest contestant to be voted off Strictly Come Dancing. The answer was Jo Wood. And my favourite birthday question completed the round – where you had to order the following by age. The musician and actress Danni Minogue, the singer Sinitta, and the actress Julia Roberts. Yes reader, a repeat of the question I asked a couple of weeks ago. But still harder than it sounds.

By this point in my quiz career I was often taking more than eight rounds with me to any quiz to give me options. And on that fateful Uxbridge evening, for our Geography second round, I had a colour photo sheet of cities, or a blank map of Europe with 10 countries to position. As the guests were very friendly, and the client had paid handsomely, I decided to run both sets to give them value for money.

I have already mentioned the TV round featuring property ladder but for round four again I had a choice. If all the multimedia was working correctly, I could dust off another of my That Was The Year rounds. This time the earliest year was the death of Winston Churchill – a funeral that my Dad marched in – and the most recent year was 2005 when Shane Warne bowled Mike Gatting with an absolute fizzer.

But in Uxbridge I was running with an audio only quiz, so we settled for sporting numbers. A sheet of facts such as Florence Griffith Joyner's record time in the women's 100 metres. And a set of 10 random numbers. You had to match the number to the fact. Surprisingly popular and a good team round prompting much discussion. Recommended.

For our music round that night it was Don't Forget The Lyrics. When the music stopped you had to write down the next line. And to help, I would provide the number of words that were needed. It was a good test of how lively the audience was because I did like to pick some very well-known songs often performed at karaoke or sporting venues.

We started with Ring of Fire, went into a bit of Take That, a touch of Amy Winehouse, a burst of Tom Jones, and finished with Cliff Richard taking us on a Summer Holiday.

The final round dusted off the Accumulator from a few weeks previously, with everyone getting apples making cider, but nobody going for the full twenty points with Tansay being a herb symbolic of mortality in Greek and Roman times.

The whole event had been superbly organised by Charlotte who worked for the oil company in question, and she had even provided prizes for the winning teams and consolations for the losers. Photos were taken, people left with big smiles on the faces, I packed up, and the tyres screeched out of Uxbridge. A place I have not returned to in 11 years.

One of my other great passions, fantasy football, saw a remarkable feat from Jermaine Defoe that week who managed to get 25 points from a single game. Luckily nobody in our league had him.

The first week of December 2009 was a memorable one. During the day I was in London for the regular job, with quizzes on the Tuesday and Thursday, and a marathon to run on the Sunday. The marathon had crept up on me and as usual I was massively under-trained, but I had managed a 20-mile training run a couple of weekends before in just over three hours so was fairly confident of getting round.

On Tuesday 1st December it was a short dart from the BBC in White City around the North Circular, up the M1, and across to the prestigious South Mimms services nestling in the bosom of Junction 23A of the M25. For cautious and nervous drivers like myself the roundabouts to get to those services are deadly, so I was pleased to make it there in one piece.

The client was on-site all day for an important team meeting and were kicking back in the evening with a big dinner in one of the conference suites. There was a 10-foot screen in the room but due to a problem with the venue projector, I was advised to take my own. It was a late start to the quiz at 9.30, but a great group made up of architects, surveyors, and people connected with property. Sadly, it had been clear beforehand that no food was to be provided for Steve. There was a distinct festive theme to both the dinner and the quiz with the teams all deciding to name themselves after reindeer.

As the quiz marked the official start of December, I had spent some of the previous weekend creating the official ask-Tony faces of the year round. This involved culling a variety of faces who had made the news, either by doing some fantastic, something incredibly criminal, or by having the misfortune to die.

Who made the cut in 2009? On the evil side there was Doctor Conrad Murray who had been involved in the death of Michael Jackson. And the Luton MP Margaret Moran who had submitted a load of dodgy expenses for housing. Famous figures from the world of sport also featured like Rory McIlroy, Thierry Henry, and Juan Martin del Potro. I liked to try and print this in colour on A3 which led to increasingly frantic hunts for an A3 colour printer. Whenever the round was handed out teams always asked for lots more copies. It was several years later, after I invested some betting winnings in a laminator, that I started to recycle this round so it lasted from late November to well into February, and the paper mountain and printer ink was cut down.

The good thing when a quiz finishes at 11 o-clock is by the time you have packed up, set goodbyes, and engaged first gear in the Black Picasso Love Wagon, there is almost nobody on the motorways. I was back home in London Luton before midnight.

Thursday the same week it was a return trip to Cheltenham to build on the success of last year's quiz visit. Cheltenham brings up tricky emotions for me as I spent five years at boarding school there. Initially my parents were in Germany so September 1982 aged seven it was a big shock one moment to go from a family lunch with my Aunt and Uncle, and Mum and Dad, to a couple of hours later being alone in a cold dormitory with a metal box containing my possessions. See you in seven weeks they said as they waved goodbye. No phone calls were allowed, although you could write one letter home a week which took place in the imaginatively named "letter-writing club" occurring after Chapel on Sundays. Once you had finished your draft, you had to take it up to the front for a teacher to read and check the contents for the following purpose:

1) If you had said anything defamatory about the school
2) To see if the letter was long enough (it had to at least stretch into two paragraphs on side two)
3) To reinforce doctrines of control and policing

As I drove from west London up to the outskirts of Cheltenham on the Thursday I couldn't help thinking about other events from those five years. Such as the time a new headmaster started replacing a much-respected former British Lions rugby player. This new headmaster quickly struck me as being a wrong 'un. Early in his reign he decided the school needed to go on a health kick so overnight introduced several changes to school food. At breakfast the next morning we came down to find no milk, sugar, or bread.

I organised a petition and by 11am the following morning over 200 people had signed it including several teachers. At 3pm I was called into the Bursar's office and advised the headmaster was not happy, but that the new food policy would be reversed. Some years later that same headmaster spent time at Her Majesty's Pleasure for much more serious offences than tinkering with the food. How anyone gave him a job in the first place remains a mystery to me.

The Cheltenham quiz that night was won for the second year in a row by Rampant Repairs who particularly enjoyed the What Happened Next round. Inspired by a Question of Sport this was a collection of youTube clips and when I stopped the action, you had to say what followed. I did not limit it to sport, mainly because the really funny clips were about other subjects. The trick when compiling this round was to try and find videos that not many people had seen.

One of my favourites is the phone-in to Manchester United Television (MUTV) where presenter Hayley is joined by legends Gary Pallister and Paul Parker. They take a call from a Simon from Leicester. Simon's timing is superb as, after Hayley introduces him, he first congratulates Gary on the size of his bulge. By using the word bulge he confuses Hayley, who asks him to repeat what he said. Simon then completes the slam-dunk by congratulating Gary on the size of his cock.

Nine other clips joined Gary in this video round – none of the others being as funny, but one featuring an African politician whose chair collapses during the interview.

Despite a relatively early finish in Cheltenham, going

home was cross-country as a decent road between Cheltenham and Luton has still yet to be built. So it was past midnight before I was back in bed, ready for Sunday's marathon.

The Luton marathon has had a relatively checkered history. Just look on google to see some irate views from runners. The race is usually staged in December and billed as the last big UK marathon of the year. It consists of three laps of the north side of Luton, with visitors joking the third lap is often run the fastest as people are keen to get out of the town sharpish.

In 2008 runners arrived to find the race had been cancelled due to a bad car accident on the A6 which featured in part of the course. The year after I ran in 2009, the race was also cancelled in 2010 due to snow. It was staged successfully in 2011 and 2012 having been moved a couple of weeks early, but then permanently replaced from 2013 onwards by a council-organised half marathon that takes place in late October.

The first two laps for me in Luton 2009 were no problem and at 16 miles I was cruising. Then the quizzes and the late nights caught up with me and I completely ran out of gas and had to run/walk most of the rest of the distance. Final finishing time was 4 hours 26 minutes. Obviously like a good proportion of marathon finishers, I immediately resolved to enter the race again to beat my time next year, but I never followed through with that pledge.

After a tiring week, there were two working weeks left before Christmas, and immediately after the marathon there was only one quiz that week. It was for a famous travel company that involves a tunnel. The theme of the party was the company 1994-2009 and it was to take place at The Drapers Arms. Three parts to the quiz, spread over dinner. A couple of weeks before the event the venue switched from The Drapers to The Brill. Not far from Kings Cross. The quiz took place in the downstairs cellar and the space I had to set up the quiz was probably the smallest ever encountered in the ten years before or since. I had to employ a chair to prop open a door to the corridor to get all the equipment in. The event itself passed off very successfully but a quick check on Google reveals the Brill closed its doors for good some time in 2011 and has now been turned into flats.

2009 ended with four events in five days. On the 15th December I was again local to Kings Cross with an event for a charity at the York & Albany pub in Camden. It was a Christmas dinner with the quiz to follow consumption of turkey and the vegetarian equivalent. The organiser was superb in providing details of the guests. Ten men, thirteen ladies. Two people had Dutch as their first language. The whole group were learning Spanish for a trip to Mexico the following year. Very kindly the quiz master was to be included for food. Our quoted fee had been reduced due to the charitable nature of the function, and for the price we had agreed to supply a trophy.

When trophies were involved Mrs Roy was delighted. It meant a trip out to Dunstable to visit the home of trophies – TT Trophies – a shop on the high road of the A5 just before you head up the hill past the farm run by cricket legend Sir Alastair Cook's in-laws.

The following day I was off to Sheffield who were celebrating their fourth booking with us. As with a lot of our best clients, the organiser of the Sheffield event was an absolute diamond, and the evening had been put together with incredible attention to detail. Catering were informed the buffet was to cover 100 people. 16 bottles of red and 16 bottles of white were needed. 200 bottles of lager. Orange juice and water. There was no way I could drink all that.

A big cliché but I had always found – in general – people in the north to be friendlier than those in the south – and my Sheffield audience were a delight. It is a hell of a drive home but in 2009 they hadn't really started digging up the M1, so it was a pretty straightforward two-hour plod listening to the great Richard Bacon on Radio Five.

From London to Sheffield and then back to London again

the next night for a quiz for a local authority. Gary Pallister's bulge made another appearance, and I ran into a good friend who used to work at the BBC but was now a big character for the authority. He proved a massive hit in the lyrics round belting out a few lines of Ring of Fire.

One night of recovery back at base followed then the final event of the year. This was at a Mercure hotel just outside Windsor and fittingly for the last engagement of 2009, the event was black tie. When this was confirmed, it involved a nervous hunt for my dinner jacket purchased back in student days, and an even more anticipated family event to see if the jacket still fitted. It did just.

The black-tie event had a complicated agenda. At 1815 the guests were to arrive at the Sandringham suite for a pre-dinner glass of champagne. They were also able to browse items that were starring in an auction later that evening. At 1835 a man was to sound a gong and guests were to enter the Banqueting Hall. A speech was to follow at 1840, followed by another at 1845, with the first round of the quiz from me at 1850.

I needed to be off stage by 1900 as it was starter time. And the chef did not want to wait. At 1925 there were some company awards to hand out. I was to pop back at 1940 for the second and third rounds. Then the first auction item. Half an hour allocated for the main course at 2020. Note a big gap between starter and main. Rounds four and five at 2050. More auction. More awards. Final round of the quiz at 2150. Even more awards and auction starting at 2200. Steve to pop back with overall scores at 2225.

The beautiful news was that I had been given the same food as the guests. Which you will know by now was very unusual. And equally unusually given that schedule, I had plenty of time to eat! Parsnip soup to start was creamy and delicious, and very parsnipy. Turkey if Pru Leith was around may have been labelled a bit dry. But the chocolate pudding to finish was the standout dish, and had Paul Hollywood been there, undoubtedly the chef would have received a warm hand-shake from the baker.

Amazingly the whole event ran almost exactly to the minute, and it was just after 11pm when I found myself back at that extremely tricky roundabout to get on the M25 and home to London Luton.

As I closed off the spreadsheet for 2009 we were down on the previous year in terms of events (62 to 73) but our price per quiz had gone up and we had focused on a lot of repeat business. And going to a venue or client who knew us meant less logistic and travel stress, and a better guest experience, as the audience knew what to expect.

Photo 13 A team on the cusp of victory in 2009

10 LES QUIZERABLES

The start of 2010 was cold. Not a surprise given it was January. So cold in fact the snow arrived and caused the first quiz event of the year to be cancelled. It was due to be a sales conference for twenty people at The Grange Country House Hotel in Bury St Edmunds. It became physically impossible to drive there on the day as scheduled as the main road out of Luton was blocked. As it was a cheque on the night arrangement, no money changed hands.

A different story the following week as the ice caps had melted and it was down to Muswell Hill in London to do a quiz for a doctor's surgery. I had noticed a trend that in some companies, particularly public sector or hospitality, the Christmas event was often staged in January when a) the rush was over, and b) the prices were cheaper. These medical people were a great bunch, although it turned into a late evening as the meal didn't start until 8p.m. as there were patients to see first.

2009 faces of the year was still going strong but as I had had some time to prepare over the Christmas break, a new set of questions had been prepared to accompany Conrad and his rogues.

Every year dawns with some uncertainty as to what money and bookings would be coming in, so Karen had hit the phones in the early weeks to see who was thinking of booking some quiz action. Anthony, who had booked in 2009, had nothing solid in the diary yet. Claire was still on holiday. Tamara had put a tentative enquiry in just before Christmas but it turned out her entire budget for the evening was £100. Andrew in Exeter had big plans for a charity event at the City Gate Hotel, but a follow-up call revealed Andy had created the entertainment himself. Chris had left the company. And Cheryl, who had booked three events in 2009 but then rung each time to cancel, made it four out of four by emailing on the 12th January 2010 to cancel the event she had booked in March

So January closed in a quiz sense with just two actual events held. In addition to our friendly doctors, we had a quiz right in the heart of London. I went back to the On This Day round as a finale but it lacked the drama of the Accumulator or Wipeout.

> Twenty-nine-year-old actor Ronald Reagan married which actress on this day in 1940?

This is a nice question but not particularly entertaining. Jane Wyman is the answer. There was also a tough birthday question trio:

> Put these three in order of age: Frank Skinner, Jools Holland, and Vic Reeves.

Vic is the youngest, Frank the oldest, but only two years separate the three.

In the day job I was in the middle of a busy project with the Winter Olympics approaching as we hit February 2010. In fact, work was so busy we had to cancel a scheduled quiz event at the Hilton Milton Keynes. This was going to be an interesting format as it involved two semi-finals and a final and was due to take place during the day with no alcohol allowed. The event had been booked via an agency for a well-known car firm, but the price had been haggled down sufficiently savagely that to take a day off to carry out the event given how much preparation was needed would not have been viable.

Another reason for swerving the Milton Keynes gig was a remarkably busy set of evening quizzes the week before, another burst of three in three days. On the 3rd of February I was in Central London at a branch of the Slug & Lettuce pub for a legal firm. The following night I was in a different Slug & Lettuce but with the same questions for a conference company. And Friday it was up to the Midlands for another visit to an annual conference I had hosted before.

For the Midlands evening I had been sent an agenda that was like previous years but with an additional note:

> Could you please emphasise, however, that we must stick to the timings. Last year there seemed to be a lot of waiting around before the results of the quiz and our Chief Executive got rather impatient!

Now from previous experience I knew this event had several variables contributing to the timings. First there were speeches from various directors. Some of which were interminably long. Then there was the speed of the chef and the waiting staff. And of course, there was how long I took to deliver a round.

I thought this year's event passed off well. The client was suffering from the effects of bringing in a new, youthful chief executive with all sorts of radical ideas. Including producing faster quiz results. As I drove from Birmingham that night, I wondered whether the new broom would book again for next year.

After the Midlands there was a couple of weeks with no events during which Karen hit the switchboard again to check on client plans. Kate wanted a quiz in the depths of the Scottish Highlands for 150 teenagers. We worked out the travel and time, quoted £1500, and understandably never heard from them again. Roz gave us a shout about an event for Cardiff University pitting alumni versus current students. Suzi enquired about an event in Aberdeen city centre. Wendy wanted a quiz at Wetherspoons in Canary Wharf but rejected our quote when she said people would be self-funding.

Now the previous year Karen had missed out on the annual trip to the Channel Islands for the financial services quiz as she was giving birth to our youngest. A deserved holiday for her in 2010 however so we flew off at the end of February for a return to Guernsey.

32 teams took part in the gala evening held at the St Pierre Park Hotel and the client had very kindly paid for us to stay the night. John's bingo from previous years had been dropped and the contest was won in a tight finish by The Untouchables just a point clear of Collas Day Conquistadors. To celebrate a busy month when we returned to Luton we went out and bought a new fridge freezer.

There was not much time to sit and admire the new chiller as March had 7 bookings. The first was for a national newspaper thanks to my good friend Craig who was still working there. Craig had some controversial views on the sporting numbers round. When we chatted a week before the event, he was of the view that the round was not very inclusive. My main issue was his chosen venue had some serious electrical supply issues as the only power points seemed to be about 100 foot from the main stage. And it was right in the middle of Covent Garden making access to get any equipment in tricky. On the night I brought with me a shedload of gaffer tape and somehow managed to rig everything up to work satisfactorily.

The key thing the newspaper understood was that for maximum enjoyment you must provide an unlimited bar. And the guests tucked in big time. It was a slightly different story the following night in Sunderland where the budget was much tighter. But for that assignment I was at home with the children. Karen had been promised a night away...

So I dropped her at Stevenage railway station for another odyssey north. She enjoyed her previous visit a couple of years ago. We learnt the lessons from that visit and booked a slightly more expensive hotel. There was no video in the quiz we provided due to venue limitations and the need to keep what had to be carried on the train to a minimum. But the guests were great fun and Karen came back the next day still the Queen of quizzing. Although she did confess she had no idea how to pronounce one of the answers. Don Quixote.

There was a short notice quiz the following Monday which had only been booked the previous week for a well-known travel company. One reason we were able to accept the booking was the location. A big hotel in central London that I knew well from my university days. The event had been booked through an agency and was exceptionally well organised. The quiz was taking place at the end of a day's conference. So the room was set up with all of the following:

> Staging & screen
>
> Back projection screen & drape kit curtains (10'x7' screen).
>
> Curtains dark blue
>
> Lectern – complimentary
>
> Hotel stage- complimentary
>
> Projection: 1 x LCD Projector (fitted with short throw lens)
>
> Audio: 1 x PA system (incl 8 channel mixer/amplifier loudspeakers & 2 x static microphones.
>
> Lectern microphone incl with PA system)
>
> 1 x Roving Microphones (for Q&A)
>
> 1 x Lapel Microphones (for presenters)

The guests had been placed into teams and each team given different hats to wear during the quiz. So we had a table with police hats, another with party hats, a third with ski hats; there were also different coloured boaters. It made the photos impressive. But the key lesson this client had learnt was again to supply unlimited booze.

You could not get a bigger contrast behind the youthful exuberance of that travel company, and the next quiz for one of the world's oldest banks. It was grey suits and work attire for an event won by Alistair's Darlings in homage to the Chancellor shortly to lose his job in the 2010 General Election. The event took place at a new bar called Bluu in Moorgate. Sadly it did not last long and today is a Fuller's Pub called The Tokenhouse. Bluu were doing a good line in quizzes as when we rung them to check the logistics, they told us they had already staged four quizzes that month. Although they had no screen or TV which struck me as odd.

It was a local event the following week as I was sent to a cricket club in Kings Langley for a telecoms firm. In almost one thousand quizzes over twenty years this event stands out. Not for the quiz itself or any of the great questions asked. Just before the final round the organiser came over and said that the team who won would win a cash prize of £1,000. It remains the biggest ever cash jackpot given away at an ask-Tony quiz night. Although the pair of air tickets anywhere in the world were probably worth more.

It was a return to Centrepoint for the big alcohol quiz towards the end of March and luckily when parking in the tight car park there was no encounters with their unforgiving concrete pillars. We were debuting a new voices round that night and the main action I took from my personal retrospective afterwards was that the voice of Peter Ustinov was not loud enough.

Peter was fixed the following week for the final event of the month that took place on company premises for a securities firm. Staged not far away from the Bluu bar earlier in the month, parking had been arranged underneath the firm's offices, and made the arrival and departure a breeze.

We were running about 10% behind 2009 bookings at the

same stage as we finished the first quarter, but there were quite a few enquiries that led to nothing. Zoe and Carl had seemed keen in their initial call some weeks previously. But a follow-up revealed their social budget had disappeared. Graham was confident his parent teacher quiz was going ahead, but our fee was too much for him. Laura, who had been a previous client, said her new managing director was not keen on quizzes.

Fabiana was extremely interested in doing a quiz for her hotel staff but didn't want to pay anything at all. Instead she said they would recommend us to all their clients. It was a tempting offer and in different circumstances given the established name we should probably have taken her up on the offer. But with several existing bookings and the date in question already booked, we said no. Michelle no longer had any budget and Louise had left for maternity. Vanessa who had seemed incredibly keen turned out to have totally lost interest.

By April 2010 General Election fever was in full swing in the last throes of Gordon Brown's government. Esther Rantzen was campaigning hard in Luton commuting from her Hampstead home. The football World Cup was on the horizon, and there was a little break from quizzes over Easter. During this period, I managed to get a nasty bout of tonsillitis but it cleared up just in time to resume questioning.

The first event was for a law firm right by The Thames. There were strong allegations of a team cheating by using Blackberries. This in the days when a Blackberry was cool and state of the art. I had managed to drive the Pablo right into the heart of Tooley Street to the firm's private garage. John from the audio visual company was providing the plasma televisions and sound system so I didn't have to worry about that. We were still going with the 2009 faces of the year, admittedly slightly rebadged as faces from the last twelve months. But thanks to the Centrepoint quiz the previous month, I had some brand new music rounds.

My twice-yearly visit to the sports club in west London resulted in a request next time for some classical music and geography. Not necessarily combined, although that might be an interesting idea. A few days later it was back to Dickens Inn at Tower Bridge for a quiz in the Copperfield Bar. That venue was still doing excellent pizzas but the sound system was the usual length of Wembley stadium away from where the quiz master usually sets up. So either you smashed out a thousand steps every time you wanted to boot up the music round, or you brought your own audio system. And even then, due to the size of the room, extension cables were required. Luckily it was in those days pretty easy to park round the back of Dickens Inn, although you then needed to negotiate some tricky cobbles to get in, which runners of the London marathon know all too well.

Even after several years hosting these quiz nights, I was still learning about speaker placement. At the next event in the centre of London I placed the speakers at the front with me, when I would have been better off with one of the extension leads threading it all the way down one side under the expensive paintings to guarantee people at the back could hear.

The news round that week showed the times we were living in. Flights had almost been grounded due to a volcano in Iceland erupting. Matt Smith was about to take over as Doctor Who. The second television debate had caused much excitement in the election, leading people to genuinely believe they agreed with Nick. A big mistake. And the London marathon had just happened, leading to one of my favourite variations on the birthday question. Put these three celebrities who all finished the marathon in order of time starting with the quickest.

Jenni Falconer 3:53

Gordon Ramsay 4:05

Ronan Keating 4:15

The World Cup was now just a few weeks away. So in the final event of the month, back again in the heart of London, the World Cup flags round made its debut. In simple terms twenty flags from countries taking part in the competition. Not the most imaginative round, and requiring further access to a colour printer as it was slightly unfair to teams to make them guess the flag from the black and white version.

A few of our prospective clients were thinking of combining the World Cup with a quiz although not many actually came to fruition. Liviana had that idea but unfortunately it did not get sign off. Matthew wanted an event back at Dickens Inn but they weren't available. Andy was a member at a cricket club in Hertfordshire and was desperate to raise some money for bats, balls, and bails, but didn't want to pay anything for the quiz. Catherine had been to a quiz of ours a few years earlier but did not want to attend any more. And Jayne who had booked before was thinking of an event in September that did not actually happen.

Early May 2010 saw no quiz activity as people were rightly concentrating on the UK General Election, and worried that the result might see the first coalition government for many years, the start of the age of austerity, and the Liberal Democrats breaking their cast-iron promise never to raise tuition fees. Luckily none of that happened.

In fact, there were only two events in May. A canal-side affair for a television company in London where the winners all got some premium bubbly. And yet another trip to a services on the motorway for a visit to London Gateway. The services event was particularly emotional as it marked the retirement after seven months active duty of the faces of 2009 round.

The general sense from my bookings manager, and love of my life, Karen was that whilst interest in quizzes was still quite high, converting enquiries into events was proving harder than ever. A glance at the May enquiry database reveals some of the problems she was facing.

Annette had been very enthusiastic but the quiz duties were now passed to Linda. Linda was waiting for the new Head of Marketing to start and advised to get back in touch in few months. Natalie had booked before and had even secured the Bell & Compass in Villiers Street in London as a venue. But a rock solid date of 20th May for the booking turned into an 11th May cancellation as the client had decided to do something else. Our man Phil who had booked before was this year told he had no social budget. Dylan who had used us for a conference had this year decided to do some other form of entertainment. Lesley was incredibly price sensitive and only had £100 spare. Jo was in all sorts of trouble as not only had her budgets been slashed but her husband was in hospital with appendicitis. Nisha had a single note more than Lesley with six crisp £20s in her hand, but there was absolutely no answer from Jordan.

Overall we were 20% down on 2009 bookings by the same stage of the year, but all was not lost. The football world cup was due to start in less than two weeks. And Esther Rantzen had left Luton after a brave battle to convince hearts and souls. She had promised Jamie Oliver would open one of his restaurants in the town, Andrew Lloyd Webber would bring one of his musicals, and perhaps most excitingly of all, Anton du Beke from Strictly would open a dance academy. With Esther's departure, the dreams of all those people also went up in smoke.

No actual bookings and a need to watch as many World Cup games as possible kept the June quizzes down to just two. A nice group of people at the Cock & Lion pub in Central London in mind June, and a law firm round the corner from Tower Bridge a day later. World Cup flags were wheeled out again, and the first question in the news round was to name the musical instrument that dominated the television coverage of the first game. The vuvuzela was the device in question. It was an exciting time for those energised by Labour leadership contests with the Miliband brothers up against Diane Abbot. And Apple fans were on tenterhooks for the launch of the iPhone 4. The 12th series of Big Brother had also just started.

Personally, as well as enjoying the World Cup I was dealing with a naughty tyre company who had gone bust after taking £150 to repair my car worn out by all the quiz miles. I was trying to overcompensate from unhealthy eating by running, and although this meant getting my 8-mile time to under 64 minutes, it resulted in another bout of tonsillitis. The net effect of the reduction in bookings was we were eating into savings, as the BBC salary was not covering increasing family costs.

So in an outdated marketing move worthy of a time ten years previous, I purchased a mailing list of the top 500 marketing directors in the UK and sent them a letter with a leaflet featuring askTony's services. Not one replied and it cost a fortune in stamps, not to mention expensive writing paper and envelopes.

There was the usual mix of nearly bookings and time wasters in the month. Matt had an event in his boardroom planned. Initially he thought quiz but then he thought no. Jill was off on a cruise down the Tyne in the afternoon with 30 colleagues. She also wanted us to supply a magician and a disco. It was surprising she did not want me to skipper the boat as well.

Susan in Bury St Edmunds wanted a quiz but her Managing Director intervened and said the staff would write the questions themselves. Clare sadly was dealing with a freeze on social events and in fact had been kicked off the social committee. There was even worse news from Christina whose company had been broken up and relocated to Basingstoke.

William had lined up a fantastic evening of entertainment in a Midlands conference centre. 100 people would have a quiz for an hour. Then they would feast on chicken and chips. Then there would be a comedian. But on 23rd June we got the news the whole event had been shelved.

For the first time in six years we had a blank month. No quiz action. This was due to several factors. Firstly, Mrs Roy was off to Croatia for a few days for her brother's wedding (no children were invited) so I was staying at home to look after our three under sixes. I was also busy at work with the end of the World Cup, and of course the general event scene was quieter as a lot of venues were using their screens for football. We were also booked for two weeks holiday in France.

The phone and email lines were still busy with potential enquiries that led nowhere. Sandra wanted something cheap and cheerful in East London. We assumed it was for the company she worked for, but it turned out it was a personal request, and whatever solution she was wanting, she knew a quiz wasn't it.

Jennifer had an overly exciting proposition and unlike Sandra, she knew exactly what she wanted. She wanted a quiz competition between several train companies resulting in a grand final in London. She then wanted to present three options to her client. Option one would be six regional rounds held in Scotland (Edinburgh or Glasgow) the North East (York or Darlington), the North West (Crewe, Liverpool, or Manchester), the Midlands (Birmingham or Derby), London and the South East (London), and Wales (Cardiff). There were to be a maximum of 6 people per team and 10 questions per round. Winners from each regional round were to go through to a grand final in London. At each event there would be a buffet dinner, and each quiz would feature 8 rounds. Audio, visual, and buzzer rounds would be part of each quiz.

Option 2 was a slight variation but with the audio-visual buzzers only present at the London final. Option 3 was for each regional event to be hosted by the people themselves with us supplying the questions. They wanted a mini website to set everything up on, and branded paper and pens. In the end the client went with Option 4 which was not to do anything.

If July was barren, August was positively bumper with six booked events thanks mainly to a group of three Cambridge events booked by the same company. Ironically the fourth of the sixth events was also in Cambridge, so it meant the chance to stay with my sister locally and enjoy an alcoholic evening.

Cambridge from Luton is an easy drive with two options. Up the A6 to Bedford and right, or across the A505 through Hitchin and Royston. The trick is not to get stuck behind the hundreds of bicycles that greet you on the outskirts of Cambridge and get gradually more numerous until you are enveloped like a swarm of bees. There is a surprising amount of free parking at the Cambridge Colleges. All you have to do is drive up to the Porter's Lodge, say you are here for a quiz event, and through you go.

After the first Cambridge event on a Monday evening at Downing College, I was back in Kings Cross on the Thursday for a great bunch of people working for an improvement company. Something to do with housing. Teams were made up of refurbishment (builders), repairs (more builders), trees services (horticulturists), and general admin (finance, performance, complaints and management). The venue was canal-side and used to staging gigs for new musicians, so was well set up with a sound system and screen.

It was back to Cambridge the following Monday where there was controversy during the Price is Right round. One of the items the contestants had to guess was a London Eye admission ticket, but I had several complaints I did not specify what type of admission so there were wildly differing guesses. The problem had been fixed by the time I arrived later that week in deepest Northamptonshire for a phone company quiz at Whittlebury Hall. It was a slightly younger, more excitable crowd that I was used to, and an extremely late start. The guests paid almost no attention to the quiz and for the first time for many years one team just refused to give themselves a team name. Loading and parking was a nightmare and took half an hour. Whittlebury was added to my dirt list of places never to visit again, although my pledge not to use the phone company has been left in tatters with a succession of the market-leading devices purchased.

Back to Cambridge the following Monday and then on to a boat in London a few days later for a newspaper group. If I had been shocked by the rudeness in Northamptonshire, here I was blown away by the friendliness, and the client gave me two bottles of champagne at the end of the night to take away.

The final events of the month were back in Cambridge, separated by that visit to my sister. On the final day of August, I found myself at the University Arms hotel parked in the disabled bay right outside the front door. That hotel has since been completed gutted and replaced by something very impressive, but for those hoping to pull off the same parking stunt, it is no longer possible.

Many people are obviously on holiday in August but those that weren't were busy getting in touch about potential future events. Natalie wanted a late Christmas party. August was leaving it extremely late. She didn't go ahead, and I was denied a visit to Fareham in Hampshire as a result. Hugo had a modest budget and his social club in Buckinghamshire wanted a quiz in September. His budget turned out to be ridiculously modest. Alex was similar. So Alex chose to write the questions himself.

In between events I spent the weekend with a bunch of 15 and 16-year-olds doing a football refereeing course with Bedfordshire Football Association. There was a moment of clarity when we were asked to watch various big tackles that had taken place in football over the past year and ask what sort of card if any we would show. One of which quite a violent studs-up challenge. 1 person said it was a red, my other 11 delegates said it was a yellow. I said I would just have issued a verbal warning. The instructor asked why. I said as the World Cup final had shown, in the early minutes of the game the referee let all sorts of challenges go unpunished. The instructor puffed out his cheeks and rose to fill every inch of his 5 foot 2 frame and said:

You laddie will never referee the world cup final.

Another dream dashed. The month saw more running than ever and an attempt to beat my half marathon record. So on the 22nd August absolutely nobody turned up to watch my crack in the Hackney Downs with a time of 1 hour 44 minutes. I celebrated with a day drinking beer at the cricket.

August was a good month financially so at the start of September after hearing rave reviews from a friend called Alan, I booked a family trip to Disneyland Paris at Christmas. A crippling financial millstone but confident that bookings in the last four months of the year would pay for it. Two weeks later in September I was starting to sweat as there were only two events in the month booked in, and several enquiries that led to nothing.

Those two September events could not have been more different. First up, a return to Beckenham to a previous client who had had their budget slashed in previous years, but in 2010 were able to afford us again. 23 teams took their seats in a competitive night once again under the stern gaze of Lady Thatcher.

What a contrast to the end of the month where I had been asked initially just to supply the questions for a massive quiz organised by a national newspaper to thank all their various advertising contacts. This was relatively new territory for askTony. First just supplying questions, and second it got us back into the world of celebrity quiz masters following the great Roy Walker five years earlier.

The budget for this event was huge, and we were a ridiculously small part financially. The newspaper was using an events company to run the whole thing. But, unusually, we were working direct for the newspaper, and not for the events company. The client wanted to vet all questions which I did not normally agree to. My thinking being I was the best judge of what was a decent question given the experience of several hundred quiz nights, rather than an organiser at a client who probably did not.

The client's initial contact had been specific. 300 guests were attending. Even male/female split. Age range between 25-50. Last year the questions were provided by an outside source, but nobody could remember who was used, hence why they were contacting askTony. All the questions would be verbal rather than video. A production company was building a stage for the event. They could potentially use a photo round which would be placed on the tables before the quiz. The news questions must contain the type of stories the newspaper featured so nothing too serious.

So we sent a quote off for £495 which was immediately haggled down to £395 as a competitor had supposedly quoted £350. I was to supply all the questions the Friday before the event. As it turned out, they only changed a couple of the photos as my original choices the client felt were too obscure. Just before the event itself we were emailed and asked to supply two people on the night to act as experts which we agreed to for an extra £150.

My assistant Mark and myself arrived on the night expecting a slick operation. Their events company had about 20 people on site but no table for their quiz experts to sit at. They had a typed script for the quiz host that ran to 46 pages. But they had no way of displaying the scores from the quiz onto the video screens they had set up. It was clear they had never run a quiz before.

A quick word on their choice of celebrity quiz host. Step forward Justin Lee Collins. To say his performance on the night was erratic would be kind. He had gained a decent reputation in the years before for his entertaining documentaries on Channels 4 and 5. I particularly liked the one where he tried to become a professional darts player. He had also hosted a lively show with Alan Carr that had good reviews.

Unfiltered though, and perhaps down to the audience profile, JLC was explicit. He opened the quiz by announcing that Bruce Forsyth had died at 5.30 earlier that day. He then screamed that he had not, and Brucie lives. He described the singer Joss Stone (who was in the news) as a something unprintable, and savaged the musical act Starsailor the newspaper had booked last year. He then linked that performance to the fact that the musician Phil Spector had recently shot himself.

During the quiz JLC went up to several members of the audience for some banter. He met one guy who said his name was also Justin. This led to about five minutes describing what Justin would like to do to Justin. Most of the people he went up to were women and he described in graphic detail what he would like to do to them later in the evening.

The musical act for the night were Toploader, famous for their hit Dancing in the Moonlight. During the quiz interval they played three songs, the last of which was Dancing in the Moonlight. At the end of the quiz my assistant saw them tucking into the free bar and said: "Toploader – freeloaders more like". Which I thought was a good line.

To be fair to JLC the audience seemed to love his chat. He struck me as a man on the edge, so much so that when I got home that night I wrote down most of the things he said. Subsequent events in his private life do seem to suggest that we did witness a man about to enter a turbulent period.

Some of September was taken up with chasing some late payments. This was unusual as most of our clients were fast, excellent payers. But the tricky mobile phone company from Northamptonshire had shown no sign of parting with cash some 6 weeks after the event. Apparently, it was to do with the person who usually deals with invoices being on an exceptionally long holiday. Our Cambridge contact also finally coughed up in the final week of September.

A few enquiries went under the radar in what was a very busy month of exchanges. Wendy wanted a quiz every week at different venues across Manchester for a period of three months. It would have been ideal for somebody who lived in Manchester. An existing client called James got in contact to say that this year they had bought their own PA system so would be writing the quiz themselves. Claire had decided to book the cheapest available quiz master and paid them £175. Sarah had a 60th anniversary bash for a branch of the NHS but no budget to play with. Paul who had booked before said there would be no quiz this year as the business was being terminated at the end of November.

A manager at the Beckenham venue had asked us if we could provide a quiz for their club regulars. When we went back with a reasonable price, she said she had found somebody who could do it for half the price. Mark was quite keen on a quiz for his school parent teacher association. His budget was maxed out at £300 which given the distance we could not match.

Perhaps the most exciting enquiry of the month was Marion who was after some nightclub quiz events for students in Newcastle, Manchester, Portsmouth, and Cardiff in the first week of October. Marion herself worked for an events company so we suspected our quote of £995 per event would probably have been trebled. So when it was presented back to the actual client it would no doubt have been smacked straight out of contention.

In October 2010 the main priority was continuing my son's education in all things Luton Town. His first game aged 5 had not gone well. We settled in to enjoy Luton v Macclesfield at 3pm and at 3.05 he asked to go home. More luck though a couple of months later as Luton won 6-1 over Forest Green Rovers and not only did he stay for the whole game, he came home smiling. A fan for life was made that day.

After some empty months October was a blockbuster with nine events mainly in the London area. The first was for my old friends at the sports club in West London who after the Easter event had controversially asked for a 50% rate cut and threatened to host the quiz themselves. A few days later I was climbing the Euston Tower via the lift for one of the highest quizzes we had done on the 21st floor. I do not like heights so positioned myself well away from the windows. It was back to sea level and another of my favourite haunts for a legal firm near Tower Bridge. 21 teams packed into their canteen for a drunken evening. A glance at the news round from that week reveals some absolute classics

> "The Aussies have picked a Sheila from Barry" was the headline when Australia chose a female prime minister born in Wales. What is her name?

The question was left over from the JLC quiz and good enough to use again. I also asked for the singer who had already had four top 10 UK singles in 2010 (Katy Perry) and the Christian names of David and Samantha Cameron's new daughter.

I had made an early start on the 2010 photos of the year so was able to give that round a premature debut. A new round had also been born containing ten short video clips from well-known advertisements that proved very popular. And crucially, thanks to YouTube, relatively easy and quick to put together.

With so many events close together I was able to use the same basic format throughout October in the confident expectation nobody would attend a quiz twice this month. After Euston it was down to Charing Cross for my regular estate agency quiz. As I knew the guests from previous years it was easy to have some great banter.

The property people were at the start of three events in

three days as the following night I was off to Cheapside for another regular customer. The big change was the venue. We had the quiz at the same place but gone was the previous manager, the pizza oven, and the sound system. In its place, a new CD player, and some microwave pre-packaged food. Luckily the alcohol was pretty much the same, so the guests left happy.

The third quiz in three nights was an overlong drive from the BBC headquarters in West London up the M40 snaking through the traffic jam to a school just on the outskirts of Banbury. The audience had been described in my briefing notes as a mixture of parents and teachers, full of yummy mummies and delicious dads.

I could barely contain my excitement as not only had I been invited to provide the quiz, but I would also be able to sit in on the annual AGM that was to take place before trivia festivities commenced. Then a curry was going to be dished out, and then the quiz master was on. It was a decent quiz and an intelligent audience. On request the final round had to be about the school which killed the atmosphere that had built up. It was a slow drive home cross country and good to arrive in London Luton safe and sound just after 1am.

Three more events in the final week of October finished the month. We started in a pretty village outside Milton Keynes at the unfortunately named Cock Hotel. An insurance broker was the client. The chef had played a blinder and dished up a hot buffet with a sausage and mash option, a lasagna, or a vegetarian chilli. For this client in previous years they had opted for a venue in Milton Keynes but this year had upped the budget and gone somewhere far more civilised. As a result, they didn't want a disco afterwards with just a polite request for some background music. It turned out the guests were so wiped out by the sausages that they had all left by the time my second song had started playing, so I was left with the main bars of Leo Sayer's Orchard Road serenading an empty room.

Two quizzes in central London completed the packed calendar and it was good to have a rest. Karen had spent most of the month on the phone sorting out all the events which ran like clockwork. But there were still people who were trying to book quizzes and not following through for one reason or another.

Sam was looking for fun party type quiz somewhere in the Holborn area in London. Negotiations were looking good but at the last minute his company decided to do something else. Nicola was very keen but the yearly quiz night was suddenly put on ice after an emergency board meeting. Sandra spoke about how very tight budgets were in her sector, and after an anxious weekend when she was catching up with her line manager for a decision, emailed back to say her event was off. Claire was eager but asked us to do whatever we could on price. Charlie wanted to get his golf club members together for a quiz but discovered that one of them hosted his own quizzes so used him instead. Tom had an area of the Pitcher and Piano in Brighton already reserved for his event, but a follow-up call revealed Tom had made other plans.

With only two months of 2010 left I was back training hard for another crack at the Luton marathon. I got up to 42 miles a week training in early November and eased off due to the six events that were on the books. We started in the Slug and Lettuce in the first week of the month. It was a venue we had used before but required quite good fitness as I had to park in the Chinatown NCP and then walk the length of Lisle Street to get to the venue carrying the PA system.

A few days later I was facing a trip to the Old Bailey. Luckily the law had not caught up with me, but we were operating a quiz for a big name in consumer goods. Representatives of all your favourite supermarket brands were there, and everyone present worked in finance. So there was no problem getting paid. Plenty of people could approve the invoice.

The next night I was back at the Slug and Lettuce. Not the same one though. A few miles to the east in fact at Fenchurch

Street. Being in the heart of the city you got the feeling this branch had had rather more money spent on it. A manager at another venue we used to use said on a good week night the city bars could take up to £20,000 in an evening. No doubt hosting a quiz helped these venues, and not for the first time I considered whether there was a way we could get a cut of whatever was drunk.

It was a welcome trip out of London next as I headed to Haywards Heath for a visit to the Chequers pub. It showed my lack of knowledge of the geography of the home counties that I always thought Haywards was on the coast next to Brighton. But it turned out not to be.

The penultimate event of the month was a visit to a Hilton hotel in Watford for a technology firm. At this time of year not only were the faces of the year in full swing, but I tended to convert the topical news round of things that had happened in the last couple of weeks. Instead it was 10 of my favourite questions about the year just about to end.

> Nude, Green Leaves and Bust sold in May for over
> $100 million. Who painted it?

This was a question written in May when the event happened. Picasso was the answer. Otherwise the last week of November was considered the turning point for the music rounds. After this time the whole quiz typically took a more festive turn. The tendency over the years was for companies to book their Christmas night earlier and earlier, but in my experience, there was nothing people hated more than festive attempts in mid-November. The earlier the Christmas booking (and in the cases of those who booked a Christmas event in January as well) typically the tighter the client, and the less fun the group of attendees.

And one night after my trip to Watford, I was inside a big Government building in Victoria for a knowledge management workshop. At one point I was stuck for thirty minutes in the underground car park. No other car was in there, and the night porter had evidently nodded off, so despite many attempts to hit the buzzer and ask him to open the doors to let me drive out, there was an eerie quiet. Just as I was contemplating a night in the car, an amorous couple who had been at the quiz entered the car park on foot from above for some privacy, so I was able to escape and go to wake the porter up.

Some of the events in November had seen the use of the quiz whiteboards extended beyond my usual Price Is Right round. I noticed that several people used to use the whiteboard during the rest of the quiz to draw pictures. So often there was a theme or a subject used as an interval round for a bonus prize or points. And not surprisingly, there were some excellent drawings which are available on the website mentioned at the end of this book.

We tended to find people telephoning or emailing about quizzes in November were generally those who had left the Christmas party organisation to the last minute. Paul wanted us to do the yearly charity quiz in Guildford. The man who usually did it was not available but only charged £100. Paul had given over a key piece of information. Their usual man was not available. We did not quote £100 but considerably more. Paul rang back a few days later to say he had found another Guildford local who was willing to quiz for £100. We wished him good luck.

Anne had an idea to an hour-long quiz for some sixth formers. She had a challenge on the budget as well as for fifty guests, each was being charged £5 which included some food. She should perhaps have joined forces with Paul, and they could have bought each guest a Tesco meal deal.

Our Cheltenham friends were unable to rebook last year's quiz as the venue had no availability. Caroline sounded keen on a quiz in Bournemouth but then quickly changed her mind. Alex wanted a fun, interactive quiz to take place during her office Christmas party which already had external caterers booked. On this occasion our fee was apparently well within budget which suggested we went in too cheap as she booked with somebody else.

After times in the year when it looked like we might struggle financially, in the end December arrived and the late surge of bookings in the last 3 months of year had occurred again, just as they had in previous years. There were six events standing between me and the Christmas turkey.

The first was a trip to the Victoria Embankment for a massive consultancy firm at a venue called the Opal Bar. Unlike many of the other London bars I have subsequently googled for this book, the Opal Bar lasted long after our quiz and actually only closed its doors at the end of 2018. When we rang to check the logistics, it was a surprise to find the only input to their screen was a DVD player based in the basement. That sounded very awkward. The helpful bar manager said their suppliers always parked on Villiers Street and walked through Embankment station to get to them.

So problems potentially with the venue and despite the multi-billion pound profits, the consultancy booking us were haggling on the price. Initially they wanted to pay 50% of what we quoted. They then raised this by £50, and finally agreed to us cutting £145 off the quiz fee. Given the evening had free champagne, money seemed to be no object. It often surprised me just how much people wanted to try and drive what for them must have been the smallest part of the cost of the evening right down.

Talking of expensive evenings, the following Thursday I was off to the Almeida restaurant in Islington for a dinner quiz for 80 people. The restaurant is not there any longer, it is now called Radici. And just looking at their website is making me hungry. There was no quibbling with our fee of £495 this time, and no wonder as the guests were settling down to a menu costing £70 per head. That is a starting bill of over £5,000 so the entertainment would cost less than 10% - even lower when you consider alcohol was on top. We were to do two rounds after the canapes at 6.45pm, and then wait whilst the guests noshed on three courses, before coming back on whenever they had finished. Towards the end of the quiz as the vino flowed, the guests were joining in lustily with the Christmas lyrics round, so I pumped up the volume on our PA system. The restaurant manager came running over apoplectic and said he would lose his licence as they only had permission to play music at a certain level from the Council.

Unusually in the second week of December I had a complete rest, which was just as well as I was ending the year with a little UK tour of four quizzes in four nights starting in the north. In the week off I managed to beat my half marathon best lowering it to 1 hour 39 minutes, a record that still stands to this day. I had only entered the half marathon because the Luton full marathon had been cancelled, a fact you the reader already knows from last year's recap.

It was a return trip to Sheffield, a city I had grown to love despite that early encounter with a vagrant. Many years later Sam and I had a proper day up there watching Luton Town take on Sheffield Wednesday and, as during my quiz visits, the warmth and friendliness of the people shines out like a beacon.

From Sheffield I enjoyed a leisurely stay somewhere local and a big breakfast before making my way to Doncaster to find that night's venue, Owston Hall. We were providing a quiz for a power company celebrating their Christmas party. It turned out Doncaster was pretty close to Sheffield so I had some time to kill and I ended up having a walk round Barnsley trying to find the Dickie Bird statue. It had only been erected the year before. A decent cup of tea at Blackburns café in Barnsley and I was on my way just as the weather started closing in.

Once again, the deal at this event was the guests were having a full 3-course meal before I was coming on with the after-dinner quiz. I had been given permission to order whatever I wanted from the hotel bar and they would add it to their bill. The audience loved the quiz and there was more great drawing on the whiteboards. For these big festive dinner quizzes, I liked to use what I considered my most entertaining rounds, so the line-up for Owston was:

In the News (from the whole year)

Faces of 2010

The Price Is Right (with interactive whiteboards)

Film Clips

Don't Forget the Lyrics

Christmas Family Fortunes

The Christmas family fortunes was a variation on a favourite I always knew went down well with a mixed lively group. Something you do on Christmas morning was the festive question, with teams having to work out the top five answers. As before, I made it topical by saying I had been out on the streets of Doncaster earlier in the day. The second and final question of the day was to name something a man does more than a woman. People genuinely love this question, it provokes laughter, debate, lots of potential answers, and more often than not, a fair degree of smut.

After a good night's rest in God's own county of Yorkshire I was on my way south to London for a charity quiz. I had enough time to stop at home and collect some new clothes. I was heading to a very unusual event. It was taking place at the Chief Executive's multi million-pound gaffe in Chiswick. The quiz was taking place in the Garden Room, but not before the guests had tucked into another 3-courser courtesy of the external caterers. The weather was chasing me south and I arrived as thick snow was covering south west London. We didn't get to ask the first question until just after 10pm but the quiz went well, and I skated the Picasso home on literal thin ice to get home just after midnight.

The final event of the year was also a quiz for a charity. They had been very keen on a round about company facts despite a warning this sort of subject did not make for great entertainment when they could have been debating what a man did more than a woman. One of their questions was what their website's visitor numbers were for November – 178,584, or 175,584.

As with any month there were events that never saw the light of day. Caroline was looking ahead to a quiz in February for 30 people in the High Wycombe area. It never happened. Laura wanted a dinner dance for some supermarket employees. But most people tend not to ask about future quiz nights in December, preferring to kick back and relax for Christmas.

There were busy spells, and some great events, but it felt a slightly less frantic quiz year. We did over 50 events in 2010, the average quiz fee dropped slightly, but there were less new clients and more repeat business.

In the final days of 2010, we went to Disneyland Paris for 3 days and 2 nights of what can only be described as the most expensive, disappointing holiday I have ever been on. The weather was brutal. All five of us got food poisoning. Large parts of the hotel we were staying in, and parts of the theme park, were closed. The advertising slogan used to state: "The magic starts when you tell them". For the Roy family, the nightmare only ended when we got home.

Photo 14 A 2010 quiz which each team wore different hats

Photo 15 JLC presenting the final scores in 2010

Photo 16 A winning entry from the 2010 bonus festive drawing round

11 BIG FACT HUNT

To be honest I was still fuming about Disney throughout January 2011. I had vented on a message board and received some consoling and genuinely helpful replies. Turned out I had booked a bad hotel. And a bad time of year. And the wrong Disneyland.

Only two events took place in January. The first was for an electricity company in Bermondsey in London. It was taking place inside their offices which were also some kind of manufacturing centre. So the venue was rearranged after I got there into a pub-style venue, and it all worked pretty well. These guys usually went for a Scalextric evening instead, so a quiz was an interesting departure. They arranged for a fish and chip van to be just outside the front and that was the food for the event. 80 portions of fish and chips in an indoor venue do make a place stink. Particularly if Trevor from accounts has gone for extra vinegar.

For the other event it was up to my second favourite city after London. And to the edge of Manchester; specifically, an area called Worsley. I had been invited up by one of the emergency services and the place was very secure. It was 11 teams of 10 people and the quiz was only for 75 minutes after which the guests would be entertained by a big band. As the trumpets were on stage taking all the room, there was to be no video round.

It was a quiet month on the enquiry front although I had some sympathy for Tracie. She had asked for a quiz in the Barbican area for 50 people. We went back with our usual rate and a few days later Tracie said she was amazed at the cost and was hoping to pay £200 maximum. Her rationale for this is she had a quiz for her school PTA some years ago and that is what the quiz cost.

Things were looking a lot busier in February. First, I was back at an old favourite The City Tavern in London. It was time to dust off a round I had not used for years in Blockbusters. Not any ordinary Blockbusters but in fact Blockbusters Valentine Special given the big day was just around the corner.

Which 'J.D.B.' was the wife of Napoleon Bonaparte?

According to an old superstition, if a single woman sleeps with what 'W.C.B.' under her pillow, she'll dream of the man she is to marry?

Ten questions of a similar ilk made up the round and, with the right theme music sound effects, it made for a decent contest. Fresh from the memory of the success of Family Fortunes in Doncaster, I had found some fresh questions and we went with these two questions for the final round:

Something you usually do once a week

A famous biblical twosome

The biblical question had a limited number of answers depending on your knowledge of the book, but the once a week question proved excellent at getting the conversations flowing, helped by the big quantities of alcohol that had been sunk. I say vast quantities but in fact the bar tab for this event was capped at £300 by the organiser which she said would allow for one drink each. There had been a pledge from the landlord that this year the platters for each team would be brought direct to their table. The reason being apparently post event last year there had been many complaints about waiting at the buffet table for stuff to be brought out.

It was touch and go whether we would go back out to the Channel Islands in mid-February as scheduled as the event was apparently low on numbers. But out we did go. Karen had managed to escape for 24 hours to join me in Guernsey where we had a lovely pre-quiz lunch at the Swan Inn. The hotel had given us champagne and chocolates which is always a lovely touch. The quiz itself was at a new venue called the Duke of Richmond, and 19 teams took part, thankfully with no bingo. This group was always very keen to play Tony's True or False which meant bringing out my 300 laminated A4 sheets putting me dangerously close to the budget airline's hand baggage limit.

It was a very quick return to the canal side near Kings Cross for the group who had enjoyed last year's event so much they wanted an early rematch. Blockbuster Valentines and the biblical Family Fortunes was still proving popular, so I saw no reason to change it. A useful geography round was added where from a list of 20 countries you had to name the 10 that were smaller than the UK in area.

There were some exciting sounding quizzes that never happened. Laura was organizing a quiz for a television wrap party in Soho. We were too expensive. Clive wanted a quiz for a Saturday night in Taunton in June. Claire in Manchester wanted to write her own questions, have her own questions, and just needed to hire from us our buzzers. Stephen was having a dinner for his club managers in Milton Keynes. We could have had a 45-minute slot to showcase the quiz, although we would have been up against comedians and magicians. Lorraine was keen on doing something at another branch of the Slug & Lettuce. But of all of them, David probably got closest. He also got invoiced. And he paid up front. We were all set to travel to Manchester for a staff away day. But it got cancelled two days before due to some major operational incident.

It had been a decent start to 2011 with just the right balance of quiz events, work, running training, and relaxing. I managed to sell an old plasma TV used for quizzes on eBay to a guy who drove down from Manchester. He asked me to help load it into his Nissan Micra, and as he put the boot down, I heard the crunch of some glass smashing. Luckily, he did not notice and drove off sharpish. In the final week of the month I did 41 miles in training which was on schedule as a few weeks ahead it would be time for the 2011 London Marathon. But first there were several events to negotiate before the weary feet once again lined up in Greenwich Park and set off round the greatest city in the world to end up hobbling down the Mall. Ten events to be precise between me and that finish line.

March 2011 was in two distinct parts. The first two weeks in terms of quiz nights were quiet. The focus was on marathon training with that London tilt just weeks away. I managed a 20-mile training run at 8 minute mile pace in the first week of March. This was then followed up with a 1:39 half marathon effort in Milton Keynes the following Sunday. Things were looking good.

The first two quizzes of the month took place at the Slug and Lettuce in Soho which was fast becoming the most popular venue for companies looking for quiz action right in the West End. In the country, excitement was building for the forthcoming wedding of Kate and William, and askTony quiz nights was not going to miss out on capturing this anticipation. So after the Price Is Right round, and often during the buffet break, teams were asked to draw a cartoon expressing their hopes and aspirations for the Royal Wedding. Some of the results are probably not publishable but I might put the best on the website after the thirty year rule for treason finishes.

Looking back at the photos of those events it is impossible not to draw the conclusion that almost everybody was drinking Magners cider. This got me thinking – has the cider craze faded in the nine years since? Whenever I have drunk Magners I have never got past the amount of sugar. But if you let 15 teams of 6 loose on the Magners, and offer them unlimited quantities, you are going to get some interesting results.

So it proved as I found myself in the Two Brewers in Marlow a week later doing an event for a marketing agency. I knew them from a previous booking and was aware it was a young, excitable, frenzied crowd, particularly after a few drinks. The landlord had the good sense to house them in his out-building. Midway through the music round people started getting up on the benches, and by the time Sweet Caroline kicked in, a full-blown food fight was underway. My first thought in these circumstances is to protect the equipment from any liquids in order of expense. At the time that meant laptop, then PA system, then projector. So I switched them off in that order. Order was restored when the fiery bar manager came running out, and the quiz was concluded in a peaceful manner.

Marlow is the sort of place I'd be happy to move the family to. If they built a couple of decent roads in and out of the town, sorted out the flood problem, and somebody gave me £2 million to afford a house there. On the way back a tanker had overturned on the M25 causing a cross-country detour and a missed long training run the next day due to tiredness.

In the final week of March, I was back in London at The Grace Bar. I had done a gig there in a previous managerial incarnation. The newspaper client was very keen on the Price Is Right and particularly anything from Argos which was moving rapidly from a print-based catalogue to online. Unusually due to client request I put the round last on the running order. By the time the audience had finished with the penultimate round, featuring lyrics from songs by John Lennon, Queen, Katy Perry, and the Kinks, the five electronics items in the closing round felt a bit flat. But nobody complained.

Several events did not materialise including Rose who wanted something upstairs at the Pembroke Castle in Primrose Hill. They decided to use their old quizmaster. Jayne wanted a repeat of last year's quiz but we were already booked on the date in question. Colin wanted a PTA quiz – and as you have probably seen before – most PTA quiz enquiries tended not to turn into quiz events usually due to budget. James was like Jane in that his chosen date was not available, and Laura told us we were too expensive.

With a late Easter there was no early April break – it was straight into more quiz action. But the big focus was on the marathon and so on the first Sunday in April I lined up at the Oakley 20, widely recognized as the last big London warm-up. A finish time of 2 hour 41 minutes gave me too much confidence. The following Thursday I was in Watford for a finance company. The Royal Wedding cartoons were still proving popular. A couple of London events followed in the next 2 weeks and then it was the time for what has proved to be my final and 11th marathon. It was all looking good until 12 miles in and then the usual blow up happened and I finished in 4 hours 17. It was still my best London time but about 40 minutes slower than the training had indicated. A 10-day holiday for Easter with no day job or quiz nights was the reward timed to coincide with the bank holidays and extra day off for the Royal Wedding.

After one long holiday, admittedly a staycation, there were only 3 working weeks in May before we were off on another holiday to France for a week. Ankle problems had developed because of the marathon, so a slightly hobbling quiz master negotiated six events in those 3 weeks. The biggest was a return to the dinner dance in the Midlands which although we had done before, was a big doubt due to the new chief executive's plans. He did decide to go ahead but not without some requested changes.

First, he wanted a string quartet to play throughout the evening to keep the mood mellow. He also did not want any video in the quiz because he thought people looking at a screen was making the evening a bit too formal. We substituted in the price is right and made the film round audio only. It worked quite well, and the chief probably made the right call for that event. Although our video film round is usually the most requested, and the highest scoring. It was quite a long flog up the motorway to the venue, the Makeney Hall hotel in Belper, but a successful night. The string quartet were excellent, although they have evidently been booked until 10pm, as at 10.01 the bows stopped, and the four ladies left the stage so quickly they missed the audience applause.

It was a positive start to the year with the quiz business 10% up year on year. We took the slow boat to France and had an overnight cabin, and arrived just in time to see Manchester United totally outclassed by the Barcelona team in the Champions League final. There was genuine hysteria in the UK in a rush to buy Olympics tickets for the following summer, so it was in those circumstances from deepest France, after a lovely bottle of Bordeaux, that I ended up buying two tickets from a German reseller for the ladies Weightlifting, just so Sam and I could say we were there.

Returning to the UK there were only two events in June 2011. This started with a first-ever visit to Beaconsfield for a travel company. Unusually it was a Monday evening. One of the guests had a birthday the same day so we had a special round about Steve. Born in the year 1974 Steve supported Wycombe Wanderers. He also has a dog called Pippa. The second event took place at Cambridge rugby club. Aside from not even knowing Cambridge had a rugby club, it was a keenly contested quiz won by just a single point. A glance at the news round shows that the country was not ready to move on from royal weddings. But we were not talking about Kate and William; this time the focus was on Mike and Zara. Mariah Carey had also just given birth to twins. And named them Moroccan and Monroe. Azerbaijan were the surprising winners of the Eurovision Song Contest.

The Cambridge event showed the potential importance of a tiebreaker which given a number of recent close finishers needed to be a corker. This month I was running with a choice of:

In what year did Starbucks first start selling coffee?

> Published in 1966 and commonly known as The Little Red Book, how many quotations are there in the book called Quotations From Chairman Mao Tse-Tung?

General enquiries were exceptionally low. Budgets had probably been smashed celebrating the royal wedding. The only tentative one we had was from Lynn who wanted a millionaire style quiz after their staff conference between the hours of 1615 and 1800 for 50 people. The original quote from us was deemed too high and after two rounds of negotiation we eventually pulled out.

There were no events in July which was just as well as I had a big new project to run at work. There was time to run a car boot sale with all the old house junk which did not actually make any money as the proceeds were spent buying the junk from other cars. Nick wanted a quiz in Farringdon but could not get the budget together. Kate had left the social committee, and they in turn had decided not to have a quiz this year. And there was no reply at all from an initial query from Emma for a quiz for 90 people at an unknown location

In August the pace stepped up a bit and for the first time I began to consider how much longer it could be sustained. First week in August I was in London on Monday for work, then went up to Cambridge in the evening for a quiz. Tuesday after work we were at the football in the evening to see a friendly with Parma. Wednesday and Thursday I was back in London for work with a quiz at Kings Cross Thursday evening. Friday I drove up to Manchester at 6am to spend the day at the BBC Salford office dropping Sam with his grandparents first. And in the evening we went to see the Paul Scholes testimonial at Old Trafford. Arriving back in the Luton in the early hours of Saturday, for good luck I had all four tyres of the Picasso changed later that day.

The following week I was back in London Monday during

the day, and in Cambridge in the evening. Three further days in London then it was off to the depths of Hertfordshire for a quiz on a farm for a major supermarket. Friday the body packed up and I was in bed with tonsillitis. I just about recovered in time for another Monday in London followed by a third trip to Cambridge, Tuesday in London with football in the evening, and then all day at the cricket on Saturday.

The ankle was still giving me problems, so I went to the physio in the final week of August. She told me to take some time off running in exchange for £38. There was still time to spend a small fortune at Costco and see United smash Arsenal 8-2.

We had helped Chris with a charity quiz a few years before but when he got back in touch his date was so close to Christmas this time we could not be of assistance. Janice could not find a suitable venue in Covent Garden. And Luke was very keen on a quiz for 100 people but eventually decided not to run the event as he ran out of time trying to organise it.

In hindsight I probably had not planned the year that well. With the holidays organised for April and May it left a long stretch to get through without a break as we went into the busiest time of year. It did look as though clients had also changed their typical plans as September 2011 was noticeable quieter than previous years with only 3 events scheduled. And crucially the rest of the year was to be negotiated with the added stress of father and son season tickets for Luton Town. A rollercoaster of emotions was therefore absolutely guaranteed. The month did not start promisingly with a 1-1- draw against Stockport conceding in injury time.

We were in Covent Garden at the end of the first week of September for a quiz for a firm who offered internet deals. The event was organised by an old friend of Redwood who beat us down on the price big time on the promise that many further events would follow for a company who was going places. As it turned out the place they were heading was down the toilet admittedly not for a few years. Their last tweet is from 22nd May 2015 urging everybody to enjoy the weekend accompanied by a picture of some sweetcorn.

That client loved the Price Is Right round which was the usual curious selection handpicked by me following a random internet surf. We had a tasting menu from a London restaurant, a used MX5 as driven by one of my old bosses, a Boston handbag, and a methuselah of champagne. One look at the news round shows these were significant times. Steve Jobs had just stepped down as boss of Apple. David Walliams had begun a charity swim of the Thames. And in Libya Colonel Ghaddafi's 42 years in power had come to an end.

There was significant news from a venue at the end of the month with a return visit to the Theodore Bullfrog near Charing Cross. The debacle with the curled sandwiches the previous year had been thoroughly investigated. For the 2011 event they were switching to hot food and the promise of fish and chips for 17 teams and the quiz master. All to be served in half hour window. It was a tall order but credit to the chef he just about pulled it off. Although the second half of the quiz was conducted under the lingering cloud of vinegar fumes.

September saw a flood of enquiries most of which went nowhere. Mariah Carey, fresh from having her twins, got in touch about a quiz in the EC2Y area with finger food for the buffet. The social committee duly met and said no. A mobile phone company wanted a post dinner quiz in Hatfield but suffered a catastrophic last-minute cut to the budget. John, who we had worked with in Milton Keynes, had this year gone for an all-in-one package that included magic show, disco, quiz, and bingo. And made the wise decision to save money. Natalie got our quote and then emailed to say she was going with someone more local and cheaper.

Krista was particularly keen to stress she wanted a quiz master with a good personality who is funny and engaging. It was all very vague with a range of dates provided and no ideas on venue. She then proved ridiculously hard to get hold of, so we reluctantly gave up.

The start of October coincided with the end of a particularly busy time at work which had resulted in a big night out in London and the emergency pulling of a tube station cord. I was all recovered a few days later for yet another trip to Cambridge and the ballroom of the prestigious University Arms hotel.

It was time to assemble the 2011 faces of the year in a round I was finding had a longer and longer shelf life each year. The previous version had only been retired in May. The stars of the new version included Pippa Middleton, Mark Cavendish, and Anthony Weiner who had to resign as a US senator for showing his weiner via photo messages to somebody other than his wife.

The ridiculously hot start to the month with temperatures touching 30 degrees saw some very bad results for both Luton, losing 1-0 to Wrexham, and Manchester United, smashed 6-1 by Manchester City. The shock was so bad I went down with a cold but got back up again to include an interesting film in the movie round for the whole month as an experiment.

Back as a student in 1994 I had missed an especially important England football game to go on a date to watch an arthouse film called The Scent of Green Papya. Very little happened in both the movie and the date, and it took a lot of searching to even track down a tiny clip of it to feature in the cinema round. It has a pretty decent rating of 7.4 on the internet movie database, but in all the October events nobody got near the correct answer.

> A Vietnamese servant girl, Mui, observes lives within two different Saigon families: the first, a woman textile seller with three boys and a frequently absent husband; the second, a handsome young pianist with his fiancée.

That is the synopsis if you want to check it out. Towards the end of the month I was in Wavendon near Milton Keynes at a golf club where I had played a couple of rounds as a teenager. The client was a leader in retail performance, and on request I had been asked to include some work questions. This included such classics as:

> In which year did the business win the Milton Keynes Citizen Business of the Year Award for Customer Service, beating off companies such as Mercedes Benz

There was another first for askTony as our final London quiz of the month ended in a pumpkin carving competition as it took place on Halloween. We didn't get any photos of it though as the judging took place after the quiz had finished and in the middle of a food and champagne fight putting the audio visual equipment at risk. So a sharp exit was made.

October was always a busy time for enquiries with proactive companies firming up their Christmas plans and 2011 was no different. Alex had an overly exciting proposal. He wanted 26 quiz nights to take place during the London Olympics in 2012. Crucially we could use the same quiz each night as the guests would be different. That original enquiry had come in January 2011 but in October 2011 Paulo had got in touch to say Alex had left and could we requote. We did, but never heard from Paulo again.

A previous client, Niamh was keen on another quiz but it proved impossible as their summer event had to be rescheduled due to poor weather. Bethany wanted a quiz to accompany a three-course meal and casino night in the Peterborough area. Nick was trying to organise something in the Canary Wharf area but we proved too expensive for him. Lynette had a big event planned for a golf club near Camberley and had already sorted a disco. Amber wanted a quiz for her Christmas staff party which was taking place in their offices. A last-minute switch saw Amber switch to an external venue where all entertainment is provided. That sounded suspiciously to me like they had decided to go bowling. And finally, Brigita had a venue sorted in St Anne's Manor, Bracknell, but wanted to start her conference week with a fun quiz. But her budget could not stretch.

In November we had 7 events booked in making it the busiest month since the unforgettable events of October 2010. Personally, I was on another unsuccessful weight loss crusade made up of a lot of running, counterbalanced by a lot of drinking and eating. We started the quiz month with a return visit to Beckenham and a decidedly average buffet. The next night it was the reassuring aromas of the Dickens Inn pizzas. A few days rest and then time once again to climb the floors of the Euston Tower and try to navigate wheeling a post trolley with three wheels containing all my equipment.

A busy final week saw three events finishing up in the grand settings of the Chancery Court hotel. This was a post-conference quiz for some lawyers. It was notable for being the first ever client to request a round of Play Your Card Right. Nine years previously I had purchased that set of giant playing cards for this very purpose. The client had also employed a staging company for the conference, and they built a very respectable game show set for the round to take place on. The food as you would expect from such a prestigious hotel was excellent.

If you added up all the lost bookings or enquiries that went nowhere you could probably run several quiz companies. Michael was after a weekly quiz in Kensington High Street which needed to be fun and interactive. Curiously he had an Australian email address. Chris had a university quiz but it was on the same night as another event so we could not help. Andrew wanted a dinner event at a restaurant in Keston. Turned out Keston was a real place in Kent.

Duncan had ideas about a team building night in Edinburgh. Jilly had a Christmas party planned for her client, but her venue would not allow a microphone or music. Jane thought about an event in Wellingborough but decided against it.

There were seven events to complete the quiz year and 2011. The two main highlights were firstly a trip to Kensington Place for a dinner quiz. The client has agreed to the quiz master ordering anything off the menu whilst he waited, to a maximum value of £15. So I settled on a nice piece of pig.

The second event was a rare excursion to the world of celebrity. A good friend who had booked a number of previous quizzes had recently moved companies, and had organised an evening for advertisers in Covent Garden. To liven up the night, the client had arranged for three big names from the world of sport to be in attendance. They were arranged at a top VIP table along with a couple of directors. One of the celebs wanted to put some music on after the quiz had finished, and so produced an iPad featuring the dirtiest screen I have ever seen.

Camilla got in touch to ask about an event taking place at the 52 club in Gower Street. Turns out that address is now a student gym. Overall December lent itself to a period of reflection, as well as trips to nativity plays and relatives. The car had cost £1,000 to fix having clocked up 70,000 miles. We finished the year with 48 events, down from 56 the year before, but only about £2,000 down in terms of revenue.

Photo 17 Action from the top of the Euston Tower in 2011

Photo 18 - Karen hosting a quiz and handing out the bubbly in 2011

12 RISKY QUIZNESS

2012 started with the usual grand plans. I was going to drink less, lose wright, eat better, and generally lead a good life. There was a lot of press chat about diets as there always is in January. People were particularly interested in revelations from the television personality Philip Schofield that after breakfast he only ate one further meal each day.

We fielded many enquiries in January and unusually for the first month ran 3 quiz events. The first was a delayed Christmas party in Battersea where the captain of each team was in fancy dress. The second was an annual quiz in the City that we did the previous year. And the final event was our first Olympics-themed quiz.

The Olympic client were holding an away day at the Runnymede Hotel in Egham for several departments who would be working on the Olympics. They wanted to use the quiz as a starter for the next few months of work. It gave me an early opportunity to put together some specific rounds that could be reused for any other clients who wanted to tie in with the big dominant event in the UK in 2012.

It was a unique quiz in many ways as the client had requested that every round be related to the Olympics so some of my favourite staples could not be included. The News round was a non-starter. Faces and photos could have worked but would have required a lot of research. There are not really that many Olympics films to make a film round. So the lineup we settled on included a music round that featured sporting tunes or songs associated with sport. There was a loose geography round linking years to host cities. And a price is right round featuring a few Olympic related items culled from the Argos catalogue.

In all three January events the amount of alcohol drunk by guests was exceptional even by askTony quiz standards. Consequently, the feedback for the month was probably the best we had ever received. I have worked for several companies who spent a lot of time analysing different metrics of audience satisfaction. Our feedback was pure verbatims and the more alcohol was served, the better the reaction.

Our first enquiry of the year on 5th January was an interesting one. Amy wanted a quiz for a client who had just invented a wireless storage device. Every guest at the quiz was to have an iPad and would answer the questions via that iPad. She stated upfront they would want their own person to present the quiz. It would also need to be very heavy on film clips and audio. We quoted high given the work involved, and never heard from Amy again.

Potential clients did seem be wanting to push the technological envelope. A day after Amy called, there was a request from Elaine who wanted buzzers on table. It was to be the evening entertainment for a conference. Elaine was intent on recruiting a professional company to run the quiz, but also wanted to insert some work-type questions.

Claire had a quiz in mind for her fun, team-building event taking place at Kuti's Indian restaurant in Oxford Street, Southampton. Our quote, which included a big wedge for travel, was way too much for her. The good news though is unlike a lot of venues mentioned to us over 20 years, Kuti's is still very much open for business. It has outstanding reviews on Tripadvisor and at the time of writing is rated the 31st best eating establishment in Southampton out of more than 550 in contention.

Barry wanted ninety minutes of fast-paced quiz action for his 40th birthday celebrations. He wanted to get kids involved and open to all ages but was unable to agree terms. Jessica wanted an event in Farringdon for her advertising agency but it was only part of the fun planned, and we were taking up too much of her budget. Natalie had a publishing client who were looking for a quiz on a Thursday sometime in 2012. The enquiry was too vague to be able to respond in a meaningful way, and Natalie proved too elusive.

In February the snow arrived, and Whitney Houston died. There was a lot of running attempted. Three events managed to dodge the snow. First it was an historic trip to Dorking. I had never been there. It was a quiz for a marketing company which had originally been scheduled for December but was postponed to deepest winter. The quiz was early afternoon and was without any alcohol. The staff had been having an all-staff meeting over lunch and this was an ice-breaker for relaxation. The Dorking crowd were a great group of people and the whiteboard cartoons were surprisingly good despite the absence of any booze-induced refreshments or even any nibbles. The big drawback of Dorking is to get home to Luton afterwards involved a long slog around the M25 which was the usual car park, and because of the event timing, I hit rush hour full on.

A similarly lively group was encountered at Marlow rugby club a week later where the organiser had ordered more pizzas than I had ever seen. To be fair the agency who the quiz was for managed to demolish the lot. Marlow saw a reworked final round called Stick or Twist which had an element of gamble and proved popular. We started with an easy question, things gradually got harder, and after each question, teams were invited to stick or twist.

> Which lasted longer, World War One or World War Two?

> Starting with the longest, list the following countries in order of the total length of their coastlines - Australia, Japan, USA and Russia

The coastline question was the toughest of the round. Nobody got it right. A week later a big bank in the City did rather better, with three teams collecting the full house of 20 points. That same bank managed to reach the venue's £500 minimum spend level within 30 minutes of the quiz starting which was a great effort.

Kevin was keen on a quiz in Watford, but we could not make it due to an existing booking. Kimberley worked for an insurance company and had £5,000 to cover a quiz for 60 people but from that she needed to pay for the venue hire, quiz, drink, and food. Kim originally put the enquiry in to us in October, and we got back with a decent quote. Then it went quiet, so Kim fired in the same enquiry start of December. Despite a progressive conversation where we recommended several venues, our proposal was never accepted, and we will never know whether the big £5,000 insurance quiz event ever went ahead.

Michelle was after a quiz in Hemel which would have meant navigating the nightmare roundabout wrongly named magic. Several years later I actually had to drive through the same roundabout on a few occasions and it turned out not nearly to be as bad as expected. The trick was not to turn right.

The final week of February saw a good friend from Hamburg visit with his fiancé and arrangements made for his wedding in Berlin which was to take place on the first day of the London Olympics. Flights were booked, hotels reserved, and the time requested off work.

March was looking busy with six events booked in before a longish Easter rest. It was a clean sweep for London town with all the events taking place at pubs or company offices within about a 4 square mile area. The first two events coincided with a busy week at work, so I took an executive decision to stay overnight in Shepherds Bush. Negotiating budget allowance with our finance director meant the accommodation booked was absolute minimum; oxygen and water facilities were paid extras; the room had a lot in common with a prison cell located right in the basement and without any natural light. How anybody could get away with advertising it as a bed and breakfast was beyond me.

A glance at the news round revealed we were once again living in exciting times. Apple had just released their iPad 3. One Direction had won the best song at the Brits for What Makes You Beautiful. Lionel Messi had scored five goals in a Champions League game against Bayer Leverkusen. Lady Gaga had become the first twitter user to pass 20 million followers. But perhaps most significantly, Engleburt Humperdinck had been selected to represent the United Kingdom at the Eurovision Song Contest. A decision that continued a proud record of failure by the selectors that continues to this day.

Kathryn spent much of the month contacting us for details on what type of quiz we could offer for her team building exercise to take place at her offices in Beckenham. Several exchanges were had and a price agreed, but it turned out to just be a fact-finding mission in case her firm ever did decide to go down the trivia road.

The start of April 2012 was probably the peak of my athletics career. I had signed up for a test event at the new Olympic stadium in London which was a 5 mile race ending in the stadium. The tagline was that you could be one of the first to cross the finish line in the new stadium. We set off somewhere in the outer Olympic park which looked half-finished. Quick, blustery conditions meant I was making good progress as we entered the stadium with about 600 metres to go. Unfortunately, I mistimed the sprint finish and was a little bit sick with about 200 metres to go. But there is a good photo of another runner who finished just in front of me being sick on the finish line which was my official commemorative photograph. 5 miles in just over 37 minutes is about as quick as I ever got.

There were 3 quiz events in April dotted before and after the Easter holidays, and they took the run of consecutive London events to 8 unbroken. The month ended with Karen and I in a hotel in the Cotswolds celebrating our 10-year wedding anniversary.

Several enquiries slipped through the net including an event for Bob in Weybridge. He wanted some quiz entertainment for his wife's 60th birthday in November. The price was not a problem. His plans just changed. Karina had a quiz in mind for 35 people in Clerkenwell. But she hardly had any budget. Elliot was working for a young Jewish charity but was similarly restricted on price. Ben was employed by a big international hotel chain and had a client who wanted a sales team networking quiz at a Holiday Inn on the M4. He had only reserved half a bar though, so it didn't seem workable. Ceri had a local restaurant booked in Warrington for 30 people but our quote was too high for her to proceed. It was the same picture for Sinead in Glasgow who went with a local budget option.

As the action moved into May 2012 the run of unbroken London events extended to 11. I also supplied questions only for a newspaper group running a quiz in Manchester. Normally we did not do just questions as clients tended to try and beat the costs right down, and there are numerous websites offering quiz questions at rock bottom prices.

The first event outside London for a long time took place in a hotel close to Horsley which meant another trip around the M25. For my money the planners have not really sorted out the roads in that part of the South East as it is pretty difficult to get anywhere quickly.

The Horsley client had been keen to include some company questions to increase the team spirit. They included:

> How many nationalities have we got attending today?

> What is our company vision?

> What is our budgeted revenue for this year?

Who is our biggest customer?

That trip south was followed pretty swiftly the following week by a visit to sunny Bournemouth for a dinner quiz at a city centre hotel. A quick walk on the beach for some chips prior to the event was followed by the quiz for a firm who were actually based about 5 miles locally to me in Luton.

The advantage of a return from Bournemouth off peak as I had found out several years earlier on Christmas Day is thanks to the all-motorway nature of the journey a rapid return to Luton is more than possible. In fact I was back home by midnight.

Kay wanted a quiz at the Reebok Centre in Docklands and although our quote was apparently very reasonable, the booking never happened. Leena had something organised at a pub in Putney Bridge but although the event was cancelled Leena emailed to say she would defiantly use us in the future. I like the idea of clients defiantly using us against management instructions not to do so. Maria wanted to have a quiz at the intriguingly named Butt & Oyster in Ipswich. Turned out the budget was only £200 for the quiz. Looking at the reviews and the menu for that pub, the client was probably right to prioritise the budget on the excellent food on offer. The seafood platter consisting of hot smoked salmon, smoked salmon, mackerel pate, dill cured herring, and focaccia, is currently on offer for just £15.95.

June and July 2012 saw only 2 quiz events as the nation was gripped by two major sporting occasions. First, we had Euro 2012. England did surprisingly well to get out of their group having drawn 1-1 with France, beaten Sweden 3-2, and getting a 1-0 result against Ukraine. Just as hopes got higher, England then dashed them all with a 0-0 draw against Italy followed by the inevitable elimination on penalties.

We had used the downtime to take a holiday in France given the slightly later than usual half term. On return there was time to see Bruce Forsyth visit the BBC for the Olympic Torch Relay, as the iconic token of the Games made its way around the country in the build up to the Olympics. My good friend Mark and I had recreated our own sporting highlight with a grudge tennis match taking place at the prestigious Westway tennis centre. Mark was pretty good at tennis and had beaten me comfortably in the last match several years previously. I had secretly been having tennis lessons from my boss Mike, a respected member of the Lawn Tennis Association.

In a one-set duel, things were not looking good when I found myself 3-5 down and love-30 on my serve. From nowhere the unreliable arm managed to conjure up four aces to pull it back to 4-5. Mark then found the pressure intensifying and threw in a few double faults to level it up at 5-5. A resurgent Luton player then comfortably held for 6-5. At 30-30 the game looked to be heading for a tie-break. I found an impossible angle to get match point at 40-30. Mark sent down an absolute thunderbolt which I got the edge of the racket to. It dollied over the net and Mark had an easy put away. Except he left it a little bit short and summoning all the remnants of the running career reserves, I picked it up inches from the line and fizzed a backhand down the line to claim a first and only tennis victory.

In emotional scenes at a shocking pub in Ladbroke Grove an hour later I announced my immediate retirement from tennis.

There was time to nip to Cambridge for another visit to the rugby club quiz. And then on the day the Olympics started it was that planned trip to Berlin for an epic wedding. The ceremony took place in a 14th century church and the reception was in the famous Pan Am Lounge high up. On the balcony for drinks the guests realised we overlooked some sort of men's sauna where all kinds of Germanic bodywork were on display.

We watched the opening ceremony highlights on the hotel

TV. A couple of days later Sam and I experienced genuine Olympic sporting drama in person. The 1,000 in the auditorium will never forget the moment when the 63 kg world record in the ladies weight-lifting was broken. The £200 I'd spent on the tickets were quickly forgotten as we became lost in what will always be remembered as one of the great sporting moments of the 21st century. Sadly, four years later it emerged that two of the competitors we had watched had been injecting all sorts of illegal substances in 2012 so their achievements were wiped from the record books.

The phone could almost have been disconnected during the sporting summer but there were a few enquiries. Chris wanted me to travel up to Leeds for an event, but Leeds is a long way from Luton. Andy had a Canary Wharf gig all lined up. The date kept changing to avoid a clash with the football. He then wanted us to send all the questions to him in advance so he could vet them for offensiveness and appropriateness. James was Bristol based and worked in a call centre so it was impossible to talk to him about his event without having to buy the insurance he was selling.

August was a little busier with quizzes as I had several Cambridge events for conferences, and a return to a farm in Hertfordshire for a leading supermarket. All events featured special versions of Tony's True and False rebranded for the Olympic year. The farm quiz had a lot of effort put into it by the organisers as the room had been dressed for the Olympics with bunting, medals, and even a menu based on the Olympic rings.

Given all the excitement of that sporting summer, September could have been a bit of an anti-climax, but it brought some new challenges. I had started working up in Manchester three days a week, which was going to prevent any last-minute quiz bookings, and also test the energy levels with an increase in travelling.

There were four events in September. Two back in Cambridge, a Central London quiz for a TV company, and a visit to

Milton Keynes back at the Cock Hotel. It was the last outing for all the Olympic rounds as people were starting to get fed up, and the Paralympics had just finished.

A ring around existing clients revealed quite a few had cancelled plans for their annual quiz to do something for the Olympics instead. Things were looking good with Laura who was 99% sure her event was going ahead, and she had even signed contracts with the venue. It turned out last minute that she asked somebody internally to write the questions instead. Julia had a big charity event in the Marriot hotel in Bristol. The legal people attending were working in a particularly stressful part of the law so it was vital the questions were kept as light-hearted as possible to give participants the maximum chance to relax. Bristol was not easy for us to get to, and no accommodation was offered by the client, so we said no.

October 2012 things were getting busy. The refereeing career had started in controversial fashion when in my first match I awarded three penalties, one of which was described by even our own boys' parents as laughably soft. The trickiest thing I found was the art of playing advantage. Too often when a clear foul went in, I was straight to the whistle.

I also spent some time looking at houses in the Manchester area in case the relocation worked out on a permanent basis. The conclusion quickly struck that in terms of value for money we were probably actually better off in Luton Town. But we resolved to continue looking.

It was clear with the schedule that some enquiries we were going to need to pass on to other quiz companies. So I met up with the Directors of QuizQuizQuiz (QQQ), the excellent quiz company we had scouted several years previously. In exchange for a small fee we came to a deal where events we could not do we would pass direct on to them. Both Lesley and Jack from QuizQuizQuiz have found fame on TV quiz shows. Two nicer people you would struggle to meet.

Juggling of the various commitments meant it was possible to do three days a week in the north whilst still managing six quiz nights in London. The first of these was our old friends near Charing Cross who had abandoned the excellent fish and chips from the previous year to return to the curling sandwiches with disastrous results for their clients.

It was time to climb once again the Euston Tower for the next quiz and an unveiling of the 2012 faces of the year. Dominated by the Olympics, the cast list was probably the best yet. Bradley Wiggins and Laura Trott were featured, the gold medalists from London, as well as less favourably, the disgraced teacher Andrew Forrest who had run off to France with a 15-year-old student.

Next up it was off to Marlow Rugby Club for an agency quiz with a welcome Dominos pizza buffet which did nothing for my continued attempts to get fitter. That same week we also supplied questions for a newspaper client. It turned out their event was cancelled but luckily our recently altered terms and conditions ensured payment still came through.

During October we managed to pass three events over to QQQ which provided useful extra income. There were some requests that neither us nor QQQ were able to satisfy though. Julia wanted a quiz for her legal partners at their London offices. A lot of the details had been worked out but a week before the format and plans for the evening suddenly changed and it was all off. A legal firm by the river were keen on a quiz but the organisation was caught up in a turf war amongst the social committee. To complicate things further, each member of staff was in a different house and they needed the results by team and house. All this seemed reminiscent of the worst kind of boarding school. I had not come across a corporate organization organised into houses before or since.

November 2012 saw us put the Luton house on the market as plans to move to Manchester stepped up a notch. The family came up to stay during half term and we took in a United game at Old Trafford. The quizzes had been quite well organised with our partnerships with other quiz firms. 9 events had been booked for November, but 4 of these were passed on to our partners, and the remaining events all fitted in with the dual location schedule.

The events I did carry out in person that month featured the debut of a musical round called number ones. I played 10 songs from the last 10 years; all the audience had to do was name the song and artist for 1 point, and for another point work out the year it reached number 1. Given the typical audience profile this worked well as often people remembered a year due it being when they got married or had a significant birthday.

The final two events of the month were the most challenging and also the most spectacular. First it was to a big venue in Chiswick for a betting company. All the guests were very IT literate and perhaps my quiz was bit analogue for them, but it went well considering the 16 teams of 10 people totalling 160 punters. The quiz took place on the same night the Chiswick Christmas lights were being switched on, meaning parking had to be round the back.

The following night, a Friday, I was at St Pancras. A station I had passed through probably a thousand times commuting into London. But we were at the grand hotel at the entrance, in one of the function rooms for partners in a legal firm. It was these sorts of events that made quiz nights great fun to host. The event had been brilliantly organised. The food was superb. Another firm was supplying all the audio-visual equipment for the conference and it was high quality gear. The audience were in great spirits thanks to the alcohol, and every round was well received.

For the first time in askTony history there were no enquiries that led nowhere in November as every request we couldn't tackle we had passed on to one of our new quiz network. It was such a simple idea and process we could and should have done it years earlier. There was enough of a price differential between companies and plenty of enquiries to go round. Some as you have seen from previous years were very price sensitive, some were not touchable due to location, and others wanted specific items like buzzers which we tended not to supply.

The final month of the year was the quietest on the quiz front for many years. This was mainly due to being up in Manchester for most of the week. In the end I did three quiz nights in the month, and passed one to a partner company. The first event was at the Beaumount Estate in Windsor for a cargo outfit. It was a big Christmas dinner with after dinner quiz entertainment. I did not get on until just before 10pm by which time everybody was paralytic. A full Christmas dinner had also been provided for me in the bar.

The annual Sheffield quiz was a lot easier to get to from Manchester than Luton, although snow in the region made the cut across the Snake Path in the dark pretty treacherous. It was the first event I remember dropping the clipboard with questions that had served me for 10 years and using an iPad instead. After the event finished, just after 10pm, I carried on back down south to Luton and got in half an hour after midnight. The tyres did a good job but the next morning the miles evidently took the toll and the right-side front was as flat as a pancake.

The final quiz of the month was taking place after another boozy Christmas lunch for an electrical retailer in a pub in Hemel Hempstead. The company had managed to get the event sponsored by a big phone supplier so the prizes – the latest mobile from that manufacturer – were surprisingly decent. A 4pm finish and a journey home of less than 20 minutes put the seal on what had been an interesting year that finished with me working in a new city, and starting to pick and choose the quiz nights that were the most fun to do.

49 events in 2012 was an increase of one on the previous year although the figures were inflated by including events we had passed on to other suppliers.

Photo 19 Wild enthusiasm at one of the Olympic quizzes in 2012

13 BUCKS QUIZ

January 2013 saw a renewed push to try and sort things out to relocate to Manchester but finding a house for our budget was proving very tricky. I was back in Battersea for the annual delayed Christmas party quiz which was every bit as good as last years. And at the end of the month I was in the City of London for another annual quiz event.

At the start of February my schedule between north and south combined to allow a window to conduct a dinner quiz back in the Hinckley hotel I had visited before. The organiser requested two quotes, one for a straight quiz, another for a quiz plus disco to midnight. Thankfully, they chose the quiz only option, as the guests did not want to land themselves with the world's worst disc jockey. It was a big event with 265 people booked in and sat in tables of 10. A few were too jaded from the all-day conference to make the quiz so numbers were down to a more management 18 teams by the time I got on stage.

We were able to pass on a request from Sally for a quiz at the Garrison pub. An event that was later switched to the Clarence. The same month, as it was looking increasingly likely we would be moving to Manchester, I met up with the guys at QQQ to look at handing over more of our clients.

March always turned to be a good month for quizzes unless it was an early Easter. In 2013 I had 5 quizzes booked in which were all carried out by me in person. Four were existing clients, London venues, and straightforward, but the fifth was a new enquiry, and great fun to do.

The client were the English cricket umpires who were having their annual conference right in the middle of the country at a conference centre in Warwickshire. The organiser was incredibly helpful at giving us the profile of all the 30 guests, so we were able to tailor a decent quiz that went well.

The line-up for the umpires including a news round with a heavy helping from sport. Ashley Cole had just won his 100th England cap. Bonnie Tyler had been selected as the 2013 UK Eurovision entry. And after 78 years, the humble iron had been retired as a monopoly playing token.

The geography round had been altered for the cricketers. I had previously run a version where you show a country on screen and ask for the neighbouring country to the north, south, east, or west. As these guys knew their English counties like the back of their hand, we did 5 questions on national knowledge.

> Which county is immediately west of Chesterfield?

> Which county is immediately south from Northamptonshire?

For the first you could have had Staffordshire or Cheshire. For the second, you are looking at Buckinghamshire. I had been tipped off the guardians of the cricket laws loved a singsong so the Don't Forget The Lyrics round had been especially selected to maximise the chances of participation. This was the playlist:

> Puppet on a String
>
> Big Bad John
>
> Sweet Caroline
>
> Delilah
>
> 500 miles
>
> Brown Eyed Girl

Hi Ho Silver Lining

China in Your Hand

American Pie

New York New York

If you ever find yourself needing ten sure-fire songs for karaoke, you won't find ten better than those.

One of my March clients had suggested an interesting variant to the joker system. For many years I had introduced the joker as us either playing the French or the Belgian system. This is something I had made up. The French system was where teams had to play their joker before the round started. The Belgian system was playing the joker when you handed the answers in, after you knew how well you had done.

These guys wanted to be able to buy another joker for £10. With all contributions going to charity. We tried it as an experiment, and nobody bought one. So the idea was dropped.

It was fairly quiet between April and June in the quiz world but things were moving up and down elsewhere. We went on a surprise week's holiday to Benidorm keeping it classy at the start of April. The surprise element was not telling Karen until 5am on the day we left. At the time we had no dogs, and no cats, so not too difficult to arrange. My mother in law Jacky packed a bag for Karen and I woke her up at 5am (Karen, not my mother in law) with a cup of tea and her passport. Just like in the BBC TV series The Apprentice, I said the car would be here in 20 minutes. Unlike the TV show, I didn't spend those twenty minutes straightening my hair. Although I would have done, had I had any left.

Several hours later we were in Benidorm on the beach. First thing Mrs Roy wanted to do was buy some new clothes as the packed bag did not contain anything she wanted to wear. It was a great week with some sunshine and a chance to relax after the north south commuting of the previous few months.

When we returned to Luton, we quickly got an offer on our house, and I found a property up in Salford which we put an offer in on. The move all looked set to go ahead. Then a survey report came back that revealed the Salford house had some serious issues, and at the same time the BBC decided they wanted to advertise for the position I was currently filling which wouldn't end in a final hiring decision until September. So the Salford house was off and the move to Manchester aborted, and I returned to work back at the London base.

There was time for one bank quiz in April for an existing client, with some big news reverberating around the world. JLS had announced they were splitting up.

> After 118 years, it was recently announced that Marin Alsop would be the first woman to do what?

Marin was going to conduct the last night of the Proms, the popular series of classical concerts at the Albert Hall broadcast by the BBC. The footballer Luis Suarez had just been banned for ten games for biting the Chelsea defender Branislav Ivanovic. That bank quiz also saw the debut of a re-worked Family Fortunes round called High Fives. Rather than a survey question where the top five answers were given by the public, this was a round featuring two factual questions with five possible answers. The debut featured these two questions:

> What five words or names from the lyrics of the Queen song Bohemian Rhapsody have at least 10 letters in them?

> According to circulation figures from March 2013, what are the five biggest-selling national daily newspapers in the UK?

It proved popular and became a goto round for various

quiz nights ever since.

Back in London permanently from June I was able to do three events all taking place on company premises. One of these events featured a good variation of the company-specific round when guests had been asked to supply baby photos of themselves. Ten random photos had been selected and teams invited to guess which member of staff was pictured.

There was less need now to pass on enquiries to partners, so we fielded a few more requests in this period. Kirsten had used us before and received quotes a lot higher from our partners, but in the end decided not to go ahead at all. Sharon was interested in a general quiz for her 165 employees, but she could not nail down a date. Rod was based near the Millennium Dome in Charlton. A previous client was not going to book anything this year as it was the firm's 75th birthday and they had a plethora of better celebrations planned. Tom worked for some solicitors in Covent Garden. Last year they had scrimped on budget and booked an amateur quiz whose content apparently was inappropriate. We quoted our rate and quick as a flash he came back to say they were going to book somebody cheaper. And Kate was looking for a quiz, but her budgets were so tight they were going to do the whole thing internally.

July 2013 I was now fully back in the Luton to London commuting rhythm and starting to enjoy the summer. There was just time to nip up to Leicester for a long services awards evening for a retailer that included a gala quiz. We were in the Grove suite at a Marriot hotel and thankfully, despite the big estate the hotel was in, it was possible to drive the Picasso right up to the back doors of the function room, unload the PA equipment and screen, park up, and set up the quiz.

That long services quiz featured a bonus question about the company between each round. These included:

What is our company's Global Vision

How many countries do we operate in globally

In which cities are our 4 UK Distribution Centres

Everybody attending was either celebrating 10 years working for the company, 15 years, or 20 years. No expense had been spared and there were some decent prizes on offer. As such, I put more thought than usual into the tiebreaker, in case the scores finished level, and decided on:

In what year did the first Wetherspoon pub open?

In what year was the fairy tale Cinderella first published?

Now as it turned out Bucks Quiz won the event by eight points so those pivotal questions went unused.

There was bad news on the email from Kate who had booked several events with us over the years. She had been ousted as the chair of her company's social committee. In my experience social committees did not usually spell good news for askTony quiz business. Where they existed, decisions tended to take longer, budgets were haggled over, and a lot more complexity was added to any proposed event.

At the start of August I had a Monday quiz in Cambridge and then it was a drive to France for 2 weeks in the sunshine. My sister and her family were already over there, so it was 6 children under 10 in a couple of mobile homes. I had a scheduled three events in Cambridge on consecutive Mondays, so the following week I left a sleeping camp for a 24-hour dash back to the UK to deliver one hour of quiz action.

The road from Les Sables to La Rochelle is not long but windy with a lot of bends. I parked up at La Rochelle airport. I boarded the propeller jet back to Stansted where I picked up a hire car. This was driven straight to London Luton to pick up the quiz equipment. It was then on the move across the A505 to Cambridge. Quiz delivered to an enthusiastic audience. At 10pm I left to stay the night in Luton and check on the garden. Next morning due to availability of flights I was on the road north to East Midlands airport. I dropped the hire car off and headed for departures. Security were inquisitive as they could not understand why I was flying alone with hardly any luggage. They did not come across many international quiz masters. By 2pm I was back in France and headed for the camp site. The whole adventure probably cost £250 in expenses for revenue of £495, but the reason for doing the trip was the events were part of a series. The client had been with us for several years, so it would not have been possible to have just two of the Mondays, as they were used to the same quiz master and a certain format.

That weekend after two weeks of prawns, sun, sea, steak, and vino, we returned to the UK and on the third Monday I was once again back in Cambridge. A few enquiries came and went. Gaynor was trying for a quiz at the Sterling bar on the ground floor of the iconic Gherkin building in London. Rachel was looking for a quiz back at Euston Tower. But a new managing director had taken over and decided to give the whole quiz over to the graduates to run. They were to oversee organising the quiz, ordering food, sorting refreshments, and writing the questions. Jason got in touch asking if we gave a discount for cash. With askTony fully VAT registered and a big supporter of the tax system, this was out of the question.

September 2013 was a significant month for the business and career as after 8 years it was time to leave the security of a permanent job and go 100% freelance. I had 2 quiz events booked in back in Cambridge, but otherwise the month was spent trying to restart the quiz business, and secure freelance work for during the day.

The new life started in October with 7 quiz events and a remarkably interesting first contract assignment in Wembley. All the quiz nights were in London and thanks to the massive Wembley car park, it was easy to get from there to the venues in the evening. Nigel Farage had announced he was once again going to stand as a MP in the general election. Sebastian Vettel was about to win his fourth consecutive Formula 1 world championship. And Glastonbury 2014 had sold out in a record one hour 27 minutes. Airport codes made a rare appearance at a couple of events as a round.

Rachel was aiming big and had booked a quiz at the Waldorf Hotel. She wanted the quiz to start at 4pm. The event had been organised following training courses the managers had attended. During the training they were competing as two teams. So she was very keen to keep the competitive element. She wanted buzzers and video Catchphrase. Sadly, we had an existing booking on the date requested so Rachel had to enquire elsewhere.

As we rolled into November the midweek quizzes led to a couple of overnight bookings at the Wembley Travelodge. Ever since I have felt sorry for any tourist or newcomer to London who looks up Wembley hotels on the internet and selects the Wembley Travelodge. Not because the hotel is that bad – it is not – in fact it is standard Travelodge stuff. The building overlooks the North Circular so it is not the most peaceful location in the world. The main issue though is the location – it is a good two miles away from the stadium and a forty-minute walk. But for a quiz master with a car on a budget it was fairly good value and ideally located.

The Travelodge stop strategy was employed to do a quiz back in Beckenham for 38 teams. It saved me about 3 hours travel time and I probably should have done it on the visits to that part of south London in previous years. The client had gone for a fish and chip supper. Given the numbers it was a quiz record for the speed and delivery of so many portions of haddock. Decent prizes were on offer as well. £200 for the winners. £100 for the second place. And £50 for third. Last place was awarded the customary wooden spoons.

A previous client at the end of November had come up with a novel approach of securing a venue. Often this was the trickiest part for a client organizing a quiz. Getting hold of a central London pub or restaurant without having to pay a big hire fee, or commit to a massive bar spend, had proved increasingly tricky over the years. But this client had solved it. They had bought the restaurant at the bottom of their building. So they had first choice whenever they needed to use it. Even better, they were able to transport their in-house PA system and AV equipment in the office lift.

December 2013 as there was considerably more money coming in to the accounts thanks to the switch to freelance, we eased off the quiz nights. This was achieved mainly by once again passing enquiries to our partners. Our only event was a dinner quiz for an old client back at the Beaumont Conference Centre in Windsor. It was the first Christmas meal of the year. You could if being ultra-critical say the potatoes were on the hard side, but the guests had got stuck into the Christmas spirit big time and the quiz went down very well.

I had extended the Wembley hotel scheme in the previous weeks to take in more than just the Travelodge so overnight visits to the Ibis and Holiday Inn were also included. The hotel selection at the time was not great given the proximity to the national stadium. But the area was already starting to get developed. and if you go to the Wembley now the place has been transformed with hundreds of flats and many more hotels now in the vicinity, as well as some decent places to eat, drink, and shop.

Photo 20 Cricket umpires loving the music round in 2013

14 THE SPANISH INQUIZITION

The number of quiz nights I was carrying out had been declining over the past few years. As usual I crunched the numbers at the start of 2014 and saw we had dropped from 49 in 2012 to 34 carried out in 2013. But as the demands of my new freelance day job stepped up, the trend was to continue dramatically in 2014.

The main personal preoccupation throughout the year was to lose weight and keep running. There was just one quiz in January, my annual visit to the City of London but to a new venue at Balls Brothers in Minster Court. Faces of the year had been prepared and there were the usual illustrious names culled from the winners and losers of 2013. Jason Duffner had won a golf tournament. Melissa Reid had been convicted of smuggling drugs in Peru. Luisana Lopilato was probably the most difficult and tenuous in that she had married the singer Michael Buble on 2011 and had their first child Noah in August 2013.

In the news for that quiz was a new film world record. The Wolf of Wall Street had just been released and set the mark for the use of the F-word, over 500 times. 16-year-old Lewis Clarke from Bristol became the youngest ever person to reach The South Pole. And Prime Minister Mykola Azarov and his entire cabinet resigned after anti-government protests in Ukraine.

About a month later I was in the gorgeous Buckinghamshire town of Marlow but not for a return trip to the Rugby

Club. The same client had this year gone upmarket and reserved a function suite at The Crowne Plaza. The age group for this event was probably mid-twenties so my recently prepared music from the last 10 years proved popular. It featured Mika singing Grace Kelly (2007), and the most recent addition was Pharrell Williams and his track Happy. The oldest selection was Toy Soldiers by Enimem from 2005.

The weight was not falling off so I hired a personal trainer at the start of March which was a big mistake. He was a good salesman and arranged for me to pay for 6 sessions up front at £30 each. What I did not realise until half-way through session 2 was that these sessions were not exclusive, and an increasing number of other customers began to start turning up. We were meant to be working on weights and stretching but his other clients were doing cardio and had different requirements. He also seemed to spend most of the session watching his female clients with a bit too much interest and his hands spent ominously jangling in his pockets. So after just 8 days into our contract I pressed the exit clause, and we went our separate ways.

There were a few more London quiz events in April and May which I managed to run although the main priority was working on the World Cup preparations for my day job. Unlike four years previously, there were no real requests for specific football rounds, and the nearest I got was to prepare a handout on World Cup host countries.

A weekend break in Munich to visit some good friends resulted in the purchase of a German national shirt for Sam which he was pleased with. This was a contingency plan in case Germany won the thing again. The excitement of the first game England were involved in quickly turned to the crushing disappointment as Italy beat us 2-1. Never mind the nation's supporters thought, we will make amends in the game against Uruguay. And that ended in disaster with another 2-1 defeat sending England home. The contingency plan was immediately actioned as Germany went on to lift another trophy with a 1-0 extra time win against Argentina thanks to Mario Gotze's stunning goal.

It was time to move on from my first contract as a freelance in July 2014, and a chance to go on holiday to France. The Picasso which had been a faithful servant on thousands of miles of quiz nights was beginning to show his age, so budgets were unleashed at the start of August. The purchase of a second car was signed off by my co-director, and a visit to a Luton Vauxhall dealer saw the attempted transaction of a Zafira. My hard-line negotiation had zero effect as when the salesman refused to budge from the price he quoted, I returned half an hour later to accept the same offer.

It was an earlier than usual summer holiday as August contained my usual run of Cambridge quizzes. It was after one of these events when I arrived back tired and emotional early in the morning that I agreed to the family request for a dog.

So that is how we found ourselves in a Bedford puppy farm in early September selecting the star of a bewildered mother's litter who had just been born. We were to collect him in 7 weeks' time once he had bonded and learnt the basics of how to cope with life in London Luton. Whilst we were waiting I popped back to Marlow but this time back to the Rugby Club as apparently the Crowne Plaza were not pleased with the state the client had left the venue in after the previous quiz.

In October there were several events to mark turning 40 including an incredibly expensive but fun weekend at the local Centerparcs. When anyone who has not been asks me for tips about Centerparcs, my advice is always the same. Make sure somebody else is paying. The people who seem to enjoy it most are the ones who go with a group of relatives and it often turns out the grandparents have settled the whole bill. We did see the former Arsenal footballer Ray Parlour whilst we were there.

I marked the move to the 40s by attempting to run 10k every day for 10 days. None of which were that fast. There was also time for an evening in London with the cricketer Kevin Pietersen talking about the launch of his book and his recent fall out with the England cricket team.

Things were getting busy at work so Karen and I took the decision to cancel the remaining quiz bookings for November and December 2014. There were only about a handful and we gave each client sufficient notice and a range of alternative quiz options that the process was well received. That did include the London sports club who had used us every year since 2005.

At home Kenilworth had arrived and was a small bundle of joy. He required two walks a night around the garden and soon got into digging up all the lawn and emptying every flowerpot he could find. Running was being stepped up, Saturday morning were spent refereeing Sam's football, and much of the rest of the year was spent trying to offset the effects off fast living. Or maybe fast quizzing?

There was no doubt as the year ended that just as my day job prospects had got bigger and better, the pace of the quiz nights in the previous 13 years had taken their toll and it was the right time to concentrate on the more sustainable career. We ended the year having carried out 23 quiz nights, down from the peak of 106 in 2007.

Photo 21 In-house legal quiz action in 2014

15 ONLY HERE FOR THE BEER

The previous chapters have chronicled by and large each year of the askTony quiz machine but it is at this point in the story that this changes. For between the years 2015-2019 the truth is that the quiz nights were very much on the back burner. We did not take on new clients, and the only quiz nights I hosted were for the people we had worked with for years who had backed askTony in its earliest days.

There was a good reason for such a drastic scaling back as the nature of the freelance lifestyle was that I couldn't be sure what I would be doing in three, let alone six months' time. And at what time the working day would finish. And in terms of location, where I would be based. There was also a financial factor.

When I was a permanent employee, each quiz night was considerable extra income that made it genuinely worthwhile. As a 100% freelancer, being paid per day was bringing in more revenue than a typical quiz. And most months involved 20 days' pay so the marginal gains of a quiz or two were much less.

2015 started with a trip to St Albans to buy some reduced Christmas decorations including a massive illuminated Santa. The running schedule was written for the month and after the usual New Year health kick, I was back down to 47 minutes for 10k.

The healthy living continued into February and by the end of the month I had run another half marathon in 1 hour 41 minutes. A few potential new contract opportunities came and went including what sounded an intriguing 3 months in Gibraltar for a betting company.

Fast forward a few months and in July I found myself taking my eldest two, Sam and Scarlett, to a 2-day Minecraft conference in London. The price of the tickets was astronomical and in truth I don't think the event was pitched at 10 and 8 year olds. We did meet some interesting game executives in the bar of the Hilton during one of the breaks in a Stompy lecture.

The same month saw a Kaiser Chiefs date night concert at Newmarket races. Race courses make for a strange atmosphere at the best of times with people with a genuine interest in horse racing mixing with people with a sole interest in getting leathered. Mrs Roy had a solitary interest in the lead singer of the Kaiser Chiefs, Ricky Wilson. Her day was completed by a chance meeting with the band in one of the back corridors of the main stand. We had got talking to a couple who had travelled down to York who had been to every single Kaiser Chiefs concert in the last 5 years, in the UK and abroad. Not only did the lady know every word of every song, she knew the nicknames and family history of the entire crew. What was a little disturbing but at the same time quite endearing was the fact that her husband did not share the infatuation, but facilitated his wife's desires out of genuine love for her.

In August for the first time in several years we did not have any Cambridge quizzes so we were able to go to France at peak time when the weather was better and the campsites busier. Too much red Leffe was drunk, but we did find an excellent French pet shop that did a great line in Labrador leads and accessories. By this time, almost a year-old, young Kenilworth had started joining me on the running paths. He quickly proved himself to be considerably faster than me, and fond of the rapid detour when either a passing dog, piece of food, or just an interesting smell presented itself. Tethered to my waist by a strong piece of elastic, the result of this immediate change of speed was often to swing me round by the hip.

A lucky escape happened on that holiday on the beach on one such run with the Kenster. We had started to accelerate when out of the corner of my eye I saw two greyhounds being led down to the sand. They were probably two hundred metres away. Literally within seconds I saw one of them approaching at about ninety miles an hour and the dog tore through the elastic and lead that was connecting Ken and myself. I thought I had wrenched my shoulder but luckily there was no damage.

There was another trip abroad in October with a half term visit to Rome. We also did a day trip to Pompeii to see the famous Mount Etna and the devastating effects its eruption had on the area in 79AD. All facts burnt into me from school, which our children had also started learning about. Mount Etna was shut for the day on our visit due to stormy conditions, but Pompeii and Naples were very much open. The guide on our tour bus was absolutely obsessed with sex and our stop in Naples included a visit to a museum boasting the largest collection of penises in Europe. This was not the most interesting or appropriate subject for children aged 10, 9, and 6 so I took the little ones around the safer parts of the museum in double quick time. In the café at the entrance my little group ran in to the tour guide, and I explained to her that my wife would be at least another hour as she wanted to study the collection in depth.

All told I did 11 quiz nights in 2015 for clients who had booked several months ahead. For the first time in over a decade no faces of the year round was produced. Nobody complained. As a consolation I introduced the general knowledge connections round which had nine general knowledge questions, with the tenth and final answer being what the connection between the previous nine is. Sometimes as a variant this was run as two sets of 5. Four separate questions with the answers connected to form a fifth answer. At least then if you struggled on the first connection, there was a second one to have a bash at. Here is a sample which we ran at the end of 2015

> In the human body, the tympanic membrane is better known by what name?

> The ear drum

> Nimble, Warburtons and Kingsmill are all brands of what?

> Bread

> The adjective "vernal" relates to which season of the year?

> Spring

> In September 2013, which British group received their third Mercury Prize nomination for their album A.M.?

> Arctic Monkeys

> What is the connection between the previous four answers?

> Types of roll - drum roll, bread roll, spring roll, arctic roll

The year 2016 arrived and saw yet another fitness machine purchased. None other than the Roger Black rowing machine. Now Roger Black was a retired successful athlete and I'm not sure what Roger would have made of his name being associated with what was a fairly flimsy piece of metal that was a very budget entry to the world of oaring fitness. My brother-in-law had gone all out with a £2,000 Concept2 rowing machine which was the real deal. The Argos beast did not last long before being flogged on eBay for a fraction of the purchase price.

It really was an enthusiastically athletic start to the New Year as at 7.15 on New Year's Day I was in the local park taking part in the special occasion 5k with other nutters. The previous evening's celebratory drinks accompanied by scallops with chilli and ginger soon made an unwelcome reappearance.

This renewed fitness attempt for the first few months of 2016 was helped by the discovery of an expensive health machine tucked away in the canteen at work that nobody used. Every fortnight on a Friday I would not eat anything in the morning and stand on the scales having taken my shoes off. Ordinarily if this was a proper weigh-in I'd have taken everything off but to stand fully naked in the BBC canteen at 0930 in the morning surrounded by executives discussing the new series of Strictly or how we could convince Vanessa Feltz to do more network TV would not have been appropriate. In 6 weeks I lost over a stone and celebrated by running a 5k in just over 22 minutes inspired by a developer called Marc. Being considerably younger, Marc was powered by limbs yet to have been ravaged by years of alcohol and commuting from London Luton.

Roger Black was replaced by a boxing stand in late March 2016 which stood like a monument to fitness in the shed until its removal also via eBay a few months later. In truth there was, and still remains, an excellent boxing gym three streets away from our house, but the prospect of being thumped in the face or body for real always proved too possible to resist. Our 14th wedding anniversary was celebrated with a night in London watching Gemma Arteton in her latest play, followed by dinner at the top of a Park Lane hotel. Not for the first time a supposedly high quality, top dollar establishment left me feeling let down badly as we were rushed through our food, none of which was memorable.

The strides made to fitness started to come undone at

the start of May with a chocolate meltdown over 12 hours caused by the delicious Fry's Chocolate Cream. Alan Partridge in his candid memoirs talks openly about his traumatic experience with Toblerone which saw him cowering in a footwell in Dundee. This was not quite as bad but the temptation of 3 Fry's Chocolate Creams for £1 was too much to resist. We were due to go to France for a week for the May half term but the French transport workers were all on strike so the trip was cancelled. Instead of the Francophile beaches we opted for the East Coast glory of Hunstanton in Norfolk, a place that became a firm favourite in the next few years.

The quest for fitness had not been abandoned. At the start of June there was a short walk down to Dunstable Road in Luton to the local bike shop and the subsequent purchase of their cheapest road bike, the Apollo Tardis or something named in a similar fashion. Keen to over spec the technology as always, I also purchased some sort of GoPro camera to attach to the handlebars. A few test outings around Luton and the environs proved successful. I even made it down the cycle route to Harpenden and back on one occasion.

Buoyed by this confidence after an early football match on the 2nd Saturday in June I set off just after 3pm for a cycle to Dunstable and back, a trip estimated at about 10 miles. The first section was easy and I arrived at the back of Dunstable in good shape. The roads then got a bit busier and it was in attempting to cross a particularly wide dual carriageway that disaster struck.

The front wheel gave way and Apollo 12 and myself fell over the railing landing in a slow-motion fashion on top of my right wrist. It felt like we were in the middle of nowhere, but as you know, we were just on the outskirts of Dunstable. I picked the bike up and talked to the occupants of a car who had stopped to see if I was OK. The wrist felt a bit strange, a combination of being bruised and a bit loose. But otherwise I was fine, and dismissing the offer of help, I started wheeling the bike down the hill towards what I identified looked like civilisation

It turned out I was in fact about halfway between Luton and Dunstable and when Apollo and I got to the bottom of the hill, we hit the main road between the two. At that point, the wrist was really starting to hurt. Half an hour earlier I had misguidedly decided to leave my mobile phone at home and instead packed a £5 note into the ill-fitting lycra. I realized I was not far from the hospital so a plan was hatched to pop into the accident and emergency and see if I could get the wrist looked at.

I didn't really want Apollo accompanying me on this trip so a visit to a newsagent was needed to a) swap the £5 for some change, and b) use that change to ring base to see if Karen could pick Apollo up. Mission was accomplished via the purchase of a bottle of water. The call was made. And twenty minutes later I was at the hospital triage, and Apollo was on her way back home in Zeus the Zafira driven by Mrs Roy with the three children in the back.

At the exact moment I arrived at the hospital, a bus crash was happening on the Luton to Dunstable busway. The medics managed to see me in less than an hour, and a fracture to the right wrist was confirmed. They put it in a cast and gave me a sling, and I decided to get the bus home.

I heard about the busway crash about an hour later after waiting at the busway stop for 40 minutes and being surprised there were not any buses. So I continued the journey home on foot and arrived home about 7pm still in the cycling lycra.

Reflecting a few hours later, and in case you as a reader every experience a broken wrist, there were a few things I noticed about having a broken wrist which I wrote down at the time:

Difficult to do up your trousers

Difficult to pick up dog poo

Difficult to wipe your own bottom

Difficult to undo a Coke bottle

Difficult to put contact lenses in

Quite difficult to sleep

You can still drink alcohol

Codeine is very effective

A cast gets itchy quite quickly

It is still possible to write the lyrics round for an ask Tony quiz night

Three days later I was in quiz action just off Trafalgar Square and did the whole thing one-handed. There was quite a bit of equipment to carry and to minimise travel I took an Uber from Luton to the heart of London and back again. So a lot of the profit from the evening was wiped out but there was no pain at all. Being left-handed meant most things were still possible although it was odd using the microphone with my left hand as that was usually held with my right.

The day after that quiz the public went to the polls for the Brexit referendum. For a quizmaster like me it showed the danger of asking the wrong question. Back at work in Manchester the following week we witnessed a real low point for the England football team as we crashed out to Iceland in the European Championship. Having watched the whole thing with colleagues in a bar in Salford Quays, and having had a few pints, I did the only thing guaranteed to calm me down in a tired and emotional state. I took a cab over to see the mother in law. A mad few weeks were compounded when the favourite Boris Johnson unexpectedly pulled out of the Conservative leadership race following Cameron's resignation. Johnson said categorically that he had concluded that having weighed up all the facts he had decided he could not be leader.

July 2016 saw Theresa May become Prime Minister. Towards the end of the month just as my wrist was getting better, Mrs Roy attempted to move a big bookcase down the stairs on her own when I was at work. The case landed on top of her leg, and she ended up visiting the same fracture clinic to be put in plaster.

This gave us a bit of a problem as it was right at the start of the summer holidays. So I came to an arrangement with my client and they very generously agreed to end my contract early. It turned out that Mrs Roy's leg was not actually broken just badly bruised, so we had a few weeks all at home together.

I was back in work the following month, and we saved up enough to afford to go Cyprus for a week at the end of October. There was a return to proper running in November and December, and in the final week of the year we added to the family with the arrival of a ginger cat called Harry. He was born with a problem with his front legs which were considerably shorter than his back legs. This meant he has always been unable to jump very high and leads to some very frustrating pursuits of birds. Which are always unsuccessful. When it comes to flies or wasps though, provided he can jump up to the windowsill via the chair, nothing escapes his paws.

Not much talk of quizzes in 2016. In fact, in the whole year I did just 2 quiz events. And in 2017, that number rose to 3. But more of that in a minute. The year did start with my January visit to the City of London for the annual quiz for the society. At home a bit too much whisky was being drunk, and I travelled to Sheffield in a failed attempt to land a lucrative piece of contract work.

Towards the middle of the year Sam encouraged me to watch all the Star Wars films in anticipation of the new release of The Last Jedi, due at the end of the year. Up until that point I had never seen Star Wars. To be fair I watched them all so close together that now the plots roll into one and I could not tell you what happens in each. The Zafira broke down in May ironically on its way to the annual service. It broke down right at one of the busiest junctions in Luton at the height of rush hour. A lot of people have a negative image of London Luton but when four complete strangers get out of their cars to help you push your battered old Zafira round the corner and up a hill into a parking spot, you know the kindness of the citizens.

Also in May there was an interesting 5k run round the local park where I met a pilot who regularly flew for Roman Abramovich. He was staying locally on a Friday night ready to chopper another celebrity on Saturday morning and had come out on a training run to practice for the following morning's park run. I showed him the course and we did a fairly fast jog for me probably at about 25-minute pace. The following morning due to over-indulging in the whisky again, I did not make the park run start line, but found my new pilot friend had finished sixth inside 20 minutes.

No French holiday in 2017 mainly due to the injuries in 2016 that had cost the family some income, so instead we went to Hunstanton again in August. The Norfolk air inspired the start of an inadequate attempt to grow a beard, which was abandoned in early October with hardly any difference to the naked eye. October also saw another of a series of 5k runs this time 15 days in a row.

The same month also saw the return to quiz action with an event for a client we had last worked with in 2014. A few months earlier in May 2017 they had got in contact simply to say their members missed the quiz master and despite the great attempts of our partner companies, they had not found a suitable alternative.

So contracts were exchanged and it was great to return to the old venue in mid October after a 3 year gap. As it was a revival by special request, the news round contained some crackers including:

> Who is the oldest contestant on the 2017 series of Strictly Come Dancing?

Debbie McGee was the answer. In the same round we asked what country Colin Firth had taken up citizenship with, due to the uncertainty of the Brexit vote. And which three-key keyboard command did Bill Gates admit recently was a mistake he would like to have changed. CTRL alt delete being the correct reply. As a twist instead of Tony's birthday question, the quiz return was marked with a political teaser for the final question of Round 1:

> According to data released recently by the Office for National Statistics, which of the following names was more popular among babies – Theresa, Nigel, or Jeremy

Jeremy was the clear winner with 54 babies, followed by 19 for Theresa, and a zero as sadly no parent in 2016 had christened their son Nigel.

In the final week of 2017, we inherited another cat. This one was from my brother-in-law. Grown up as a stray in the mean streets of Manchester, she was a perfect non-sexual partner for Harry, so we christened her Meghan. Before the year was out, she demonstrated hunting prowess her ginger friend could only dream about by ripping a bird to shreds in the garden and bringing in several parts of the animal into the house to show off her trophies.

From a quiz count of two in 2016, to three in 2017, we went up to nine in 2018 and to some glamorous locations. But the year started in a similar way to previous ones with another concerted attempt to train for a London marathon. January training went well including a weekend visit to Newcastle to see some football that featured a Sunday morning trot along the Tyne. In Hunstanton a month later there were several evening runs down the promenade past the lighthouse. A half marathon in March in 1 hour 57 showed things were just about on track, followed by the longest training run of 18 miles in just over 3 hours. But a week later left knee pain surfaced and I booked an appointment with a specialist using my new Vitality health insurance. So on London marathon day I dressed in my running kit but watched the race on the television in the living room, before sharing a bottle of wine with Mrs Roy and sending my relatives some pictures of me lying on the grass outside with a previous years medal round my neck captioned with the words "just finished – exhausted!".

We had carried out two quizzes at the end of January / start of February, then our return to West London at Easter. But there was a new client who had booked on the recommendation of the West London club. So, it was in late April I found myself at Jamie Oliver's corporate headquarters just near Arsenal's stadium. It was an after-work quiz in their offices for the various parts of his business. Incredible to see the different parts of his empire, ranging from books, to TV, to restaurants, to mobile apps, and it was a lesson in entrepreneurship.

The specialist in May said there was no real problem with the knee but instead the left hip had some osteoarthritis that was probably genetic. He advised against any more running and said I would be better off making lifestyle changes rather than having any surgery. So on holiday in France for the May half-term after unwisely forgetting his healthy living advice for the evening, I ordered an expensive smart bike to a) replace the running and b) overcome the safety problems I had associated with outdoor cycling ever since the wrist incident.

That bike lasted about as long as the Roger Black rowing machine though was considerably better made. I also did not make much of a loss on it as I managed to sell the bike privately to a physiotherapist in the Midlands who was going to use it to assess his patients. It went to a good home and Mrs

Roy was pleased as a massive shiny black stationary bike no longer took up half the living room.

One of my oldest and favourite clients had expanded their quiz nights from their Central London base in 2018. As a result, I was invited to ask the questions for their offices in Jersey in June, and for their partner conference in Gleneagles in November. Arriving at Glasgow Airport on the Saturday afternoon I went to the Hertz car hire kiosk to pick up the Vauxhall I had reserved. Unwisely I had also opted to wear a shiny light blue suit that had been purchased from eBay. Seeing this person walking across the terminal the salesman had obviously thought we've got a bit of a chancer here. So he tried to sell me an upgrade to a Porsche Boxer for just £60 extra. The agreement had been the car hire could be added to my expenses so I said no. Which was probably just as well as when the guy gave me the keys to the Vauxhall, I sat in it for twenty minutes trying and failing to switch the thing on. It turned out there was a red button marked ignition which did the trick.

Back in Luton the following month it was time to say goodbye to one of the oldest servants of askTony quiz nights who had been faithfully by my side since 2007. Pablo the black Picasso had reached the end of her road. Trying to do the right thing and send her off in dignity, we took her to the Citroen garage where she had been purchased. The cheeky swines attempted to charge us £100 for the privilege of taking her. So Karen cleverly rang Philip Schofield instead and his WeBuyAnyCar outfit took one look and paid us £250. A look on DVLA a few weeks later saw Pablo had received a face lift and was back on the road and is probably bringing many more miles of motoring pleasure to her owner.

2019 began in similar fashion to 2018 with a lads trip to Newcastle to watch some more football. Recovering a day later an Irishman knocked on my door with an interesting opportunity. He and his gaffer had been doing some tree work up the road and had some spare capacity. Would I be interested in having my trees trimmed in exchange for £200 in cash? If so he would bring the van and his tools straight round. He would need the money that day so I would need to visit a cash machine.

Five minutes later I expected a proper building van with a logo down the side and a couple of trained operatives. Instead his wife rolled up in a battered plain transit. Never mind I thought, he will soon be up a ladder with his chain saw doing his finest. I next saw him with a cigarette hanging out of his mouth having climbed up a bay tree hacking the branches with what looked like a rusty kitchen knife.

Forty minutes later he claimed he was done but the trees looked in a right state and after a few threats to call the police I gave him half the money and told him to get lost. What mental aberration had happened to persuade me to book him I still try to work out this day. The only consolation was thinking of my friend Bob who shortly after university was walking home in East London when a man stopped him to say he had two world class speakers in his van and would he like to buy them. Thirty minutes later Bob had been walked to the cashpoint, withdrawn £500, and was the proud owner of two speakers, each the size of a small man. What was odd about this story was Bob did not have a sound system, and the speakers remained unused.

Maybe there was an obsession with vans because a month later in Hunstanton Mrs Roy and I found ourselves seriously thinking about buying one. Not to drive around houses cutting trees down, but to visit as a static holiday home. In the end we did the sums and decided the monthly maintenance was probably not affordable, and there were also concerns about the entire Norfolk coast getting eroded by global warming and our van being cast adrift out in the North Sea.

In April there was a proud moment as AskTony became a true family business as Scarlett came along to the West London members quiz to act as scorer and assistant quiz master. She was also able to add a much needed youth element to the questions including my pathetic attempt to pronounce the name of the upbeat singer Billy Eilish. I went with Irish and Scarlo was straight on the microphone to tell me it was "Eye-lish". We also took the opportunity to pose in front of a £250,000 supercar parked outside the venue.

Sixty days without alcohol followed that quiz until we got to our summer holiday which was a week in a beautiful farmhouse in Wales. I am not sure whether it was relaxing in the hot tub or Mrs Roy's purchase of one of Lidl's finest reds, the St Emilion Grand Cru that usually retails for £10.49, but within an hour we were each two glasses in.

Highlight of that holiday apart from the peacefulness and tranquillity were the morning visits to the top of the hill to visit two horses, a mother called Boris and her young son Nigel. On our first visit the Roy family, being very comfortable with horses, saw these two animals racing over and immediately sprinted out of the field, with two of the team trying to vault a six foot gate. But it turned out that the thoroughbreds were just thoroughly hungry and on subsequent visits a few pieces of carrot and apple went down incredibly well. A swift google revealed the secret was not to stand directly behind or in front of them. Given the size of their eyes they were best approached from the side.

A month prior to Wales and right in the middle of the abstinence was a return trip to Jersey for quiz action. Jersey is very much an island favoured by retired couples and young, amorous couples, so it was interesting the following day to wonder around the island to various pubs, and drink nothing more than coffee and the excellent Fever Tree tonic water, although not together.

Pablo needed replacing but I was not willing to commit properly to another vehicle so during the year I leased two replacements. First was Alfie the Citroen Aircross who was with me for 6 months. He was really a big cousin to Pablo but had some modern gizmos including the digital screen featuring Android Auto. The rental company tried to increase

Alfie's handling fee after 6 months by £100 a month so instead I downgraded to Filipo. Filo was a black Fiat 500. He was driven down to me by a Yorkshireman who rang when he was about twenty minutes away to tell him he was close. His voicemail went down in office legend:

> Mr Roy – just to let you know I will be with you soon, ready to drop off your *little* car

Filo also had a digital screen but was considerably bouncier on the roads, and not as reliable. Even though he was only with me for 3 months, Filo still managed to suffer a driver's tyre puncture, a situation no doubt quickened by the mad number of roundabouts in Milton Keynes where I was working.

As the year and decade finished, I made my third trip of the year to the Champions League winners and Premier League champions-elect Liverpool to carry out some corporate training. The increase in the amount of this training over the year I was doing during the day led to a new employment opportunity so reluctantly I handed my notice in at Milton Keynes and prepared for a new role in 2020 delivering Agile training and coaching around the UK and Europe. Quiz nights were becoming increasingly part of the past. Or so I thought.

Photo 22 A Champions performance in 2018

16 THE QUIZ WHITTY CREW

2020 dawned with just two quiz clients left on our books. Our comrades in the West London sports club who had been with us since 2005. And our friends just off Trafalgar Square, who also started with askTony in 2005.

But it was the day job that was poised to dominate the year. January was my final month working on contract terms in Milton Keynes, and I resolved to spend it getting there by bus, just as I had done at the start in October 2018 before renting Alfie. The pledge to use the bus lasted two days before I remembered how horrible it was. Smoking is obviously not allowed on buses, but what I noticed about long distance bus travel, and I am counting the thirty miles to Milton Keynes as long distance, is that almost every passenger smokes outside the bus before they get on. Unless you are on a very luxurious bus, almost what you would call a coach, there is extraordinarily little air circulation, so the stale smoke from clothes just permeates the interiors as the months go on.

The upside of bus travel though is the price. For a week commuting to Milton Keynes the price was less than a day return to London by train. Most of the passengers appeared to work in Milton Keynes shopping centre. Only a few of us carried on the extra mile or so to be terminated at Milton Keynes Central Station.

The car I rented for the final two months in Milton Keynes was so unmemorable that I cannot remember the make, and I am writing this just a few months after I rented it. What I do remember is my visit to the concrete cows in MK a couple of days before leaving. The cows bring a certain amount of notoriety to the town, and in truth many of the residents seem ashamed of them. There are in fact two sets as the original set became too vandalised to be left open to the public, so they were moved to a local museum. The ones I was visiting though were just a couple of miles from the station and looked relatively easy to find by a combination of bike and foot. So I hired one of the famous bikes from outside the station, and set off.

About forty minutes later I was a bit lost in the countryside having negotiated two forests, a graveyard, and a particularly rickety bridge that crossed a canal. But Google had not let me down, and one further river crossing later, I had arrived at the cows. The shame the town feels for the creatures was further heightened by the lack of any signs to help people find them.

The start of February 2020 saw me swap the glamour of Milton Keynes for a one-day visit to the Slough headquarters of my new employer. During the early weeks, my schedule for the rest of the year started to take shape. I passed some early training tests and accreditations and looked at the calendar ahead.

There was a lot of London-based classroom training scheduled, but a fair amount of European travel to Dublin, Amsterdam, Paris and several secure looking military bases. Fast forward to the middle of March and I was doing my last training observation before the big schedule kicked off.

I was doing a 4-day course in Tower Bridge the week starting March 16th when word starting to get round that we were heading for some sort of lockdown with the coronavirus spreading swiftly.

The rest of the course was delivered from home having agreed with my employer given the circumstances it made more sense.

The national lockdown was then confirmed a week later

on the 23rd March. That week, along with the rest of the UK and the world, I was coming to terms with the new reality. The children were now all off school, and it was time to embrace working from home for us all.

Over the evenings in that week amongst a lot of other thoughts my attention went back to the quiz nights. I sent an email to my 2 remaining clients asking if they would be interested in running a quiz event to keep their people together and keep spirits up. One client was dealing with a lot of other work changes caused by the pandemic, but the other client put it to the members who were very keen.

This was confirmed on the Thursday, so I had 2 days to do some tests and get the technology and format right. My family were very patient and agreed to take part in several trials. I chose Zoom to connect the guests, and Kahoot to load and run the quiz on. In the testing it became clear each person needed 2 devices to take part in the quiz. One to watch the quiz, and the other device to answer the questions.

So on the 27th March the first ever askTony virtual quiz was held. The advertised start time was 7.30pm. 193 households had logged on to Zoom to take part in this moment of askTony history. I had loaded up 100 questions in multiple choice format. They were all a random assortment of topics, as to be honest I had spent most of my time working out the Zoom and Kahoot technologies.

The best move was having my son Sam act as the quiz producer. We had two chairs at the desk in the study, and he had his own machine to operate. I loaded Zoom and Kahoot on my computer, shared the screen, and then he logged in to Zoom with his own headphones. This gave us the ability to see and hear what the guests would experience. He could also monitor the Zoom chat and respond to any questions contestants might ask.

There were quite a lot of technical issues in that first ever quiz. The main concern was that a lot of guests did not know how to use Zoom or were very new to it. Using Kahoot on a different device also caused some problems. A few contestants you could see and hear via video asking somebody else in the house to help them with technology.

The other main area of difficulty was the difference between an actual quiz and a virtual one. For these guests, when we were all together at a venue, the people sat in teams. I asked the question, the team conferred on the answer, and the captain wrote the answer down on their sheet. At the end of each round, I would collect the answer sheets for each team. We then got on with the next round, during the gaps in which I would mark the papers and show them the scores from round one.

That is how a quiz worked for almost twenty years but here in the Zoom world it was all different. First the team concept did not really apply. People were playing individually as households. Secondly, there was no gap for marking, as Kahoot did the scores instantly. Kahoot allowed several different formats for questions. The most popular was a picture or video question where you could enter up to four possible answers. You could also do an open text answer question. You could get the contestants to arrange up to four different answers in the correct order. And as well as quiz questions, you could ask surveys of the audience such as what were they all drinking, to get instant feedback.

There were a few lessons learnt from using Zoom as well. First, I had not selected the "mute everyone on entry" option, which meant as the hundred guests arrived, everybody got a cacophony of noise. And second, I had allowed anyone to screenshare. Sure enough, within a minute of me starting to speak and introduce the quiz, somebody had taken control and drawn a willy on the screen.

Another issue that first quiz uncovered was my own computer was seriously underpowered. It took ages to start up and was slow drawing the video windows of all the households on Zoom. So I took an executive decision to order a new laptop. The other thing that became apparent was I needed an extra monitor. For quiz nights it was useful to have several things open as well as a view of what I was sharing by video. For my work training courses, a second monitor also became a necessity.

Another test event was required and on Tuesday the following week it was Mrs Roy's birthday. Due to lockdown the planned spa break with her best friend in Reading had been cancelled, so she was forced to attend a special birthday Zoom quiz instead. This had been organised for 4pm and invites sent to her parents, brother, and local friends.

That birthday quiz also revealed some more useful insights. A couple of the people arrived late at about 4.15. Not really a problem given the low numbers for the birthday, but if it happened at a paid quiz with hundreds of people it probably would not work. Another guest tried to access the whole thing on what looked like the world's oldest iPhone. She arrived online, did not put herself on mute, and spent two minutes saying she couldn't hear anything, before signing off.

The next virtual quiz, event 2, was for my other client. They had asked for a trial event for their marketing department to see if it would scale to their whole company, and overseas offices.

Taking the lessons from the first event, I reduced the number of questions to 70, and put them into set rounds. So, we had News, Geography, Music, Observation, Movies, and Nature. The quiz went well, although as numbers were only 8, the banter and atmosphere were perhaps a bit lacking. The actual Kahoot quiz lasted 52 minutes, so with the introductions, and end of quiz chat, the whole thing was just over an hour.

Event 3 was for the original client. I had limited time this week and it was still an experiment, so I cut the quiz right down to just 47 questions. What I noticed for the first time in this event was how apprehensive I got about the broadband failing at my house. There was no contingency so if it went down, we would be snookered. A plea went out to the rest of the house to stay off Netflix when a quiz was on.

One thing I had not settled on was whether to stage breaks during the quiz. In Kahoot I had loaded the whole quiz as one set of questions which had the advantage of giving just one set of scores at the end. But in event 3 halfway through I gave the audience a 10-minute break to chat and refill glasses. It proved a disastrous mistake. For when I pressed Next Question on Kahoot at the resumption, Chrome responded with a memory error, and promptly crashed.

This gave Sam and I our first experience of what felt like a major crisis. The quiz had failed. We had no choice but to reload Kahoot and restart. What we in fact did was scroll manually through the questions that had already been asked. Although we asked people not to answer the first lot of questions again, inevitably some people did. Eventually we completed the quiz and afterwards I had to match up the second set to the first set of answers. Some people had also changed their name between the two groups.

The fourth quiz event, and the final free one, was given to my banking friend to get his staff together. They were only a small group of 7, but it was perhaps the best quiz so far. The technology worked perfectly, and we had been able to customise a lot of the photos and questions with pictures of the contestants at various parties. We also had our first international guest, as one person joined from Germany, and another was outside in the sunshine. So it did prove you could take part from anywhere.

Two weeks into lockdown and word had spread about the Zoom quizzes and I was starting to get bookings from people who had been at the test events and told their friends. Not being in the office and everyone working remotely was in its early stages. Whereas at a real quiz people would want it in the evening with drinks, I got a few bookings for 4pm in the afternoon, others for 6pm, and some for 8pm. So these three slots were established, with the 8pm taking a slightly higher price tag.

On the 9th April I did an event at 4pm for an investment firm, and an event at 6pm for a bank. The following night we did a test event for a chain of country clubs, whose venues had been forced to close by the outbreak of the pandemic. And a day later on the Saturday we did the third of our weekly quizzes for our west London sports club.

Already in this new wave of virtual quizzes, a few patterns were starting to emerge. Whereas with a quiz in a pub or office, you did not really notice a few latecomers, in an online quiz it was run live, and as host you couldn't really wait for people who were late. In a pub, chat would flow naturally person to person. In an online video group chat, that did not really happen. If I was doing an event at 4 and one at 6, I couldn't have the first event overrun otherwise I wouldn't be able to set the second one up.

Where people took part in the quiz from also varied dramatically. As did the device they used to access the event. Some took a casual approach and dialled in via the smallest iPhone they could find. Then when the questions were displayed on screen, they complained they could not see the photos or video. Others took advantage of the great weather to sit at the end of their garden in a hammock. This resulted in frequent disconnections as they were on the boundaries of their Wi-Fi signal. We had one guy who joined the quiz from the car on his way to Asda for his weekly food shop with his kids.

In the case of the sports club we had an audience of quite differing ages and tech savviness. The good thing about doing a series of weekly quizzes for these guys is you could see people learning to use the technology better week by week. From hearing stories during the week, it emerged that children / neighbours / friends were helping anyone struggling get connected to Zoom, get the right speaker / microphone setup, and the best place in their home to access the quiz from.

For any new client the instructions were proving quite hard to simplify into a format that was easy to email, and easy to understand. I had a lot of help from our first few clients with feedback and managed to put a PDF together with basic instructions. The key message to get across was that any guest had to register via a Zoom link. And that for the quiz they needed 2 devices. A big one to see and hear the quiz and other people, and a smaller one to enter their answers on.

On Monday 13th April we ran our 8th paid virtual event, for another London sports club. There was still some experimentation going on with the right length for the quiz. The test events people felt were too long at 80 or more questions. For this one we cut it to 50 and went with that format for the rest of the events that week.

There was still a bit of a banter problem in those first few events. After the disaster of stopping for a long break halfway that led to the earlier Chrome crash, I didn't want to put many breaks between the rounds as I usually did for actual quiz nights in pubs. People generally used this time to go to the bar and get the drinks in. At home we were finding people generally had the bottle with them on the table, so drinks breaks were not needed.

But we needed to break the quiz up, so it all lasted a bit longer, and some of the social aspects of a real event were retained. We had the Zoom chat window enabled which led to some comments. Most tended to be questions as to what the Kahoot pin code was. I tried in the opening introduction to let people know about the "raise hand" feature on Zoom, and if people used it, we would visit them at the end of the round. The trouble was a lot of people had not got to grips with that part of Zoom. Sometimes we asked people to wave if they were OK for us to go live to their home. It turned out people who waved usually had a technical problem they wanted us to fix. A couple of client contacts just said – visit any house you want. If their camera is on, they are fair game. The trouble with that system was when we did go live to a house that was not expecting us, one of a number of events tended to occur.

First, there was some sort of sound issue. Either they were using several laptops to connect to the same quiz, or they were using a WhatsApp or Facetime link to broadcast the quiz to other families. Whatever the method, the result was bad hissing feedback as my voice echoed back from the several speakers in their home whenever I tried to speak. The other issue that presented were people did not know how to unmute. So we couldn't hear them. Or they were busy doing something else. One regular quiz household just appeared to consist of a sleeping dog and a completely empty living room.

Eventually after a number of these early events, the best approach was to agree with the organiser a list of people who would be fair game to have a bit of banter with between rounds. And the other clue I picked up was the seating position and camera quality of the contestants. If they were bang in front and in focus, chances were they had good audio, decent broadband, a quality camera, and would be fabulous to talk to. If they had a bottle of wine half drunk in vision, they would be even better to visit.

In those early quizzes the finish also tended to be a bit of an anticlimax. We would declare the winners, play a bit of victory music, have a chat to the victorious house, and then thank everyone for coming. Turn off our camera and the microphone, fade up the closing music, and after 27 seconds, close the connection.

A proper quiz needed a proper ending. So we decided to involve the animals. At most houses it was clear some sort of pet was sharing the house. Often a dog. Cats had been spotted. One guest in the earlier quizzes had a teddy bear as a mascot. So we put some appropriate music and invited any animals in the house to join us for the musical finish. It proved to be an extremely popular feature. All ages in the house joined in. It also had the effect of lengthening the quiz past a full hour.

We were getting bookings flying in now as word continued to spread. I was still doing some remote training with my day job. The home office had undergone some hasty improvements. The main job was to evict Harry the Cat whose favourite sleeping place was on the wooden chair with the big cushion facing the window. A movable desk from Costco had fortuitously been installed several months previously. A rummage on eBay found another expanding desk to accompany it, as did the purchase of some magnetic whiteboard paper so I could plan various training events and quizzes on the walls without permanent damage.

50 questions were lengthened to 60 and between each round we also asked a series of survey questions to get a picture of what was happening. Questions included what is everyone eating tonight, what is everyone drinking, any TV or boxsets you can recommend, a hobby you have taken up in lockdown, a book you couldn't live without, a song you'd take to a desert island, a celebrity you'd invite to the dinner, and the first thing you would do as soon as lockdown was lifted. The survey results were displayed instantly on screen as people typed them in and made for a decent discussion point. We also started to include photos that clients had sent in to feature during the quiz. At the end there was an option to suggest a subject for next time. So we were getting quite a good picture of what was working, and decent feedback on how the quiz could be improved.

The biggest test yet came on the 17th April when the country club asked us to run a quiz and invited most of their members. My system with Zoom and Kahoot had been extended to cope with 500 video participants and up to 2,000 quiz entrants. But when registrations went through 600, I panicked and bought capacity for another 500 on Zoom. As it turned out, 400 joined us online for the quiz by video, with 368 successfully completing the event. But because of the extra costs I made a loss on the evening. Luckily the client was very understanding and agreed to an increase in price for the following week.

With big numbers, it became a little bit more difficult to identify the round winners and visit their houses because Sam & I were faced with a sea of 400 video thumbnails and a wide range of player IDs. And with such large numbers, there were a few more reports of people having difficulty using the technology. From my earlier events I estimated about 10% of people registering would not actually make it to the actual quiz.

I was also conscious that for a lot of people this was all new stuff. Not just in having to cope with the rapid conversion to video conferencing. But the total absence of their usual hobbies, whether it was going to the cinema, meeting at the pub, or simple pleasures such as seeing family. With the country in an unprecedented state of lockdown, the quizzes were, if done right, providing a tiny bit of comfort in an increasingly uncertain world.

And so the feedback we got from that first mass event of 400 people ranged from people very, very cross that they could not get the technology to work, to people who emailed immediately after the quiz finished to say how much they enjoyed it, and couldn't wait for next week.

The rest of April settled into the pattern of having the two big quiz events on Friday and Saturday nights. There were some guests potentially attending both, so I would write a new quiz during the day on Friday, and then write a brand-new version for the Saturday event.

Using the topic requests from the survey results, and now with the knowledge that a 6 round, 60 question quiz with the musical finish lasted around an hour, the settled format became the following line-up:

Topical (In The News)

Mixed Bag (Topics suggested by the guests)

Sport or Food and Drink (depending on audience profile)

Music

TV & Film

Double Points

The Double Points round was a new addition as in some events we were finding the leaders had pulled too far clear to make the finish exciting.

For each quiz I was getting complete data on how every guest had answered each question, how many seconds they took to answer, and obviously what they typed into the survey questions. It did allow better customisation of future quizzes. And it showed patterns in what topics the guests asked for.

Whenever I did a quiz that did not feature a geography round, it was always the most popular suggestion in the survey. In those early virtual events, the winner usually got an accuracy rate of about 70-75%.

We also got a picture of things people were doing during lockdown that represented wider trends across the country. When faced with the question "what's the most exciting thing you'll be doing this week" one group's most popular answer was sleeping. Drinking, cycling, and gardening also featured highly. When asked for what new cooking challenge people would be attempting in the week ahead, correspondents most popular answer was toast. But we also saw banana bread, sourdough, pulled pork, and an ambitious baked Alaska.

What I also noticed from the repeat events was as people were getting used to the format and technology, complaints massively reduced. Numbers never hit the 400 again for the big Friday quiz, but that meant a lot of the more negative comments disappeared. Presumably if you could not get it to work the first week, you just didn't register for future events.

Our most international quiz yet took place at the end of April for a firm who had guests joining from New York, Stockholm, Luxembourg, and Paris, as well as employees all over the UK. It was the 21st virtual quiz we had carried out since lockdown had started just over a month previously.

By the end of May that number had doubled to 42 virtual quizzes. As well as our regular Friday and Saturday events, we did our first family event for a client who had relatives in 3 different continents. The format worked as well for a group of 7 as it did for 400. What I did find is with 7 people you could run the whole thing a little bit more relaxed on the timings. The small events I could also leave "open miked" so people could talk during the questions. At the bigger events leaving so many microphones unmuted would have been unworkable.

We were very happy to help a charity who had had to cancel their actual pub quiz at a pub that had been closed by the pandemic, and which was always a big fundraiser for them. The quiz moved online, and the team managed to match what they raised usually by using a JustGiving link we promoted before and during the quiz, and an online raffle that was drawn at the end of the night.

For a new client that worked in property with people joining the quiz from locations all over Europe, we had a great addition to the musical finish. One of the guests disappeared down his drive in Yorkshire and as the music played, his camera zoomed straight to one of his sheep.

In the early days I was always incredibly nervous about my broadband going down during the quiz and leaving everyone disappointed. But as the number of events without any incident grew, this worry got smaller.

As the format got more defined, it also became more straightforward to write the questions for the quiz. A lot of online sites were awash with their own list of pub quiz questions, which I didn't want to repeat. But there were plenty of specific film, TV, and geography places I could visit to get ideas. And thanks to youTube and my archive of existing questions from the previous 20 years, it did not take that long to put 60 questions together.

What did take time was to proof and test I had put the questions in correctly. For video questions that meant the youTube link still worked, and I had selected the right time codes. It meant checking the correct answer had been specified, and for the double points round I had indeed doubled the allocated points. Given the volume of events, I was also careful to check I had not asked the same question the previous week. Each Zoom meeting also had to be set up correctly, with screen sharing for guests off, annotations off, and computer audio selected.

As the number of events grew, I also became more conscious of the different experiences guests were having during the rest of the week. Some were working from home. Some were not working. Some were retired. A few had just had babies. At most of the events we had people working on the front line in the battle against the pandemic. Doctors, nurses, delivery drivers, and pharmacists all featured. At one fundraiser in mid-May we had a team who were actively working on one of the vaccines.

You also had a big variety of family units. People in big kitchens with a lot of space. Flat mates cramped into a small space. Some nice gardens with hot tubs visible. Tenth floor flats with no outside space. A lot of people with small children. More than a few with teenage children. And people back living with their parents having previously moved out.

In June we were getting towards three months of lockdown and I noticed a general feeling of Zoom fatigue. Those working from home were spending most of their day on Microsoft Teams or Zoom equivalents, and a few of our guests had taken part in multiple family quizzes. There were also a lot of competing Zoom activities from traditional events that had moved online. People were doing Zoom Zumba, Zoom acting classes, Zoom theatre, and even Zoom speed dating.

The other noticeable thing that happened in our regular events is a few guests got a bit more obvious with their cheating. In a traditional quiz I usually relied on self-policing. If a team of 6 was on google or their phones during the quiz, often the other teams would call them out and the offenders would be shamed into stopping. What was happening at the virtual events was more sophisticated.

The most obvious tactic was just to switch your camera off. Then when the question came up on screen, nobody else could see if you were on Google or Bing. A more elaborate ploy was to have a bank of other screens or devices connected to other members of your team. So any question could be discussed and the right answer agreed upon.

What was much more transparent with the virtual events though was the data could conclusively prove who had been cheating. The downloadable results from Kahoot gave reaction times from every contestant to every question. People who answered quickly were more likely to have attempted a genuine answer. You could also see patterns where a contestant got most of the first half of the quiz wrong. Then their camera went off, and lo and behold, the rest of the quiz the answers were all perfect.

None of the 2020 events featured prizes so my attitude to any cheating was relaxed. If people wanted to play it that way, they could. If participants numbers were low, and everyone was on screen, there was little point every trying it.

What was good though was that even with some up to shady deeds, the winners each week of the regular quizzes still tended to change. On occasion if the winner did look particularly suspect, I put up on screen their answer patterns and reaction times to each question, so it was pretty clear what they were up to.

For some events we turned off the chat feature as some of the comments were getting a bit offensive. Instead the focus went back to finding out what was on the menu. One Friday we had guests who had spent the afternoon salt baking some trout. Another family were having lasagna, a second group were feasting on milk bottles, and one family had just got out the cheese board.

Towards the end of June I did another free event for my ex colleagues from Milton Keynes, some of whom had moved on to pastures new. What was interesting about this quiz was it gave me a first-hand example of the difference in social interactions between people who used to sit next to each other in a cramped office, and who were now talking on Zoom. Every one also had different experiences of lockdown, from two colleagues who had just had babies, and had been robbed of some of the joys of new parenting like visiting relatives, to older parents who had not seen their adult children for four months.

Our weekly Friday quiz towards the end of the month was dominated by the presence in the musical medley of two bunny rabbits live from their hutch – another quiz first. One of the cockerpoos was also feeling sorry for herself having been stung by a bee.

In total June saw another 10 events, which took us to 51 in just three months. Rumours were starting to spread that the end of lockdown was getting close, and with the weather heating up, July just saw the continuation of the Friday quizzes right up until the country clubs could reopen on the 25th July.

At the final Friday weekly quiz, which had run for 15 weeks since April, we had quite a lot of fun visiting some of the best guests and animals from the previous weeks. Numbers had dropped from the 300 finishers from week 1, but we still had over 100 who made it all the way to week 15. There was some fantastic feedback as well from people who said the quiz had helped to get them through lockdown.

That final quiz had been slightly overshadowed by Luton Town's remarkable escape from relegation to secure Championship football for another season. In June, our former managerial hero Nathan Jones, who had controversially taken the money and run to Stoke halfway through a previous season, returned to lead us to glorious safety. All was forgiven. It gave me as excuse to add Nathan Jones by Banarama to the pre-quiz playlist. Nothing could displace the most appropriate song of lockdown, Living in a Ghost Town by The Rolling Stones from being played in the four minutes seventeen seconds leading up to the quiz starting:

> Life was so beautiful
> Then we all got locked down
> Feel a like ghost
> Living in a ghost town, yeah

There was just a handful of events in August and September as most people scrambled to Eat Out to Help Out and grab 50% off food courtesy of Rishi Sunak. But at the time of writing in October 2020 with infections increasing rapidly, the winter looks like a time when more people will be back in some sort of lockdown in their houses or flats.

It will be interesting to see whether there is any further demand for virtual quizzes over the winter. It was clear during the first 2020 lockdown that people were craving social company. And that after the first few weeks of eager adoption of Zoom and the novelty wore off, people got a little bit fed up of having to do pretty much all their social activities over what was, and still is, quite a narrow communication medium.

Yes Zoom, Microsoft Teams, Google Meet, and the rest, can cross national borders and link individuals, families, and companies in different continents. But the nature of the format still made it quite an individual, solo participatory experience, without the joys of meeting people face to face, enjoying a drink, and experiencing the other senses near each other.

17 I GET LOCKED DOWN, BUT I GET UP AGAIN

After twenty years, quiz nights are as popular as they have ever been. The lockdown of 2020 has seen almost all of them move online. Quiz shows on the television continue to be well watched. The BBC show Pointless has just finished its 24th series.

But are there any secrets to putting on a good quiz night? Based on my experience over the years, you are welcome to follow all, any, or none of the following tips.

Get the right venue (1)

When restrictions are over, and we go back to actual quiz nights where people meet face to face, the right venue is key. You want a dedicated room where your guests can be as loud as possible. You want decent food and drink. Beware any pub that just bungs stuff in a microwave. Avoid pubs that only serve Sam Smith's lager.

You need a venue with a modern PA system, and that means as a host or organiser all you should need to bring is a laptop or even just a phone. The venue should have a microphone for you. I prefer handheld microphones as I can shout into them or whisper and use them as a prop. Others prefer headset or lapel microphones. If you are genuinely going to entertain the crowd, you need different voice pitches. If you notice in stand-up comedy, most performers prefer to use a hand-held microphone.

Check your venue and the seating so there are no dead spots from the speakers. I have done a few gigs where a couple of teams are sat in corner where the venue didn't bother to put a speaker. The host will get it in the neck.

One of the biggest improvements in venues over the years has been in the video equipment. When I started you were lucky if the location had a television. If it did, it was often wired to a DVD player in the basement. Gradually TVs improved to include HDMI leads, then plasmas were replaced by LEDs, and in some venues TVs were networked to allow one device to plug in to multiple screens. Some places still use projectors. If yours does, make sure they have replaced the lamp sometime in the last century. Many times I have done the whole quiz with a red "lamp warning" end of life sign on display.

If the whole quiz is online, choose your video conferencing system carefully. There is now a wide range to choose from with Google Meet, Microsoft Teams, and Zoom probably being the most well-used. When your numbers get above 100 is normally where the cost starts to mount, and you need to be sure of a decent broadband connection.

Know your audience (2)

Before any quiz I speak to the organiser about the audience who will be coming along. The typical questions are the age range, nationalities, gender split, do they all work together, and any specific info relevant to the night. Sometimes the quiz takes place on a birthday or special occasion, or on a few occasions, on the night somebody was leaving. It is a bit cliched but if there is a high male ratio to the audience, I normally put a dedicated sports round in. Because if I do not, it is the area I will get most complaints. If it is an international audience, I will not put any British TV themes in the quiz.

Virtual versus physical quizzes have the biggest impact in terms of matching the quiz to your audience. When people have been confined to homes, we have often had families participating. That affects the music and film rounds, as you need a decent cross section to cater to tastes. Possibly the most difficult quizzes I have had to run are where you don't know who is going to attend, and you don't know the ages. Bournemouth on that Christmas Day quiz stands out. We had teams ranging in ages from over 80 to under 10. Had it been online I would have planned for that given it was likely to feature family groupings; because it was an on-site quiz and open to the public, the organiser had no-idea how many or who were going to attend.

Stick to a format but make it varied (3)

This might sound contradictory, but in both types of quizzes I run, virtual or physical, I tend to use the same basic format but with a variety of question types. The advantage is if you get repeat bookings, some of your guests will become familiar with their favourite rounds and look forward to them. It also makes the questions slightly easier and quicker to write, as you are more accustomed to the style.

As an example I start with an In the News round, and in that round I will do a few verbal questions, a couple of audio ones where people might hear a person's voice or a piece of music, and a couple of visual queries. It allows for a bit of banter about the events of the week and warms the audience up as you get to know them. It also acts as a good test of the standard and type of crowd you have got in. Some individuals and teams are particularly good at current affairs, but rubbish at more academic subjects like geography or science. Only rarely does a team winning after the first round go on to win the whole quiz. In fact, I think it has only happened 9 times in askTony history, although if a team does continue to lead into rounds 2, 3 and onwards, I always refer back to that statistic and just change the number.

Following a news round, if I am at a venue, I will do a picture, video, or audio round as the second round. This gives me the time to mark the answers to the first round whilst the guests get 5 minutes to complete round 2. This then allows me to read out the answers to the first round and show the scores within a 15-minute round window.

On that basis my standard 8-round physical quiz lasts about 2 hours without any food breaks. I can flex the time to run it more quickly if I need to tie in to set food deliveries the chef has requested.

Round 2 for a virtual quiz will tend to be a mixed bag of requests the audience have requested before. There is no gap for scoring as the scores are displayed on-screen immediately. By and large depending on the banter between rounds my Zoom quizzes tend to last one hour or 10 minutes per round.

Virtual quizzes will have a sports round in the round three slot, with music at round four, tv & film at round 5, and a double points round to finish. Venue quizzes you have got a bit more flexibility to insert whatever rounds you want, but I tend to always have a geography round, a mystery round, and a sports round. The tv and film round is a banker, and the music round the most popular.

Decent questions (4)

This is the most subjective area of any quiz. One person can think a question decent, another will undoubtedly hate it. With vast numbers of questions and answers now freely available on the internet, I think the trick is to mix your own creations with ones you know have worked well before.

If you are short of time there are a number of websites where you can download questions for free, and another set of resources where you can buy complete rounds pretty cheaply. For my quizzes as I have run so many events, I have a good database of questions and rounds I can potentially re-use, including over 100 audio and video rounds.

Do decent questions mean questions you cannot google? Depending on your attitude to cheating, it may do. A straight knowledge question is the easiest to google. Which of the Spice Girls is the oldest? Extend it a bit such as Which of the Spice Girls Got Married First and even if you are using google, you lengthen the time it takes to find the correct answer. A

Who is This Photo question can now be detected by Google Lens, and What Song is This can be answered by Shazam. Put these four films in the correct order again takes longer to check with Google, and if you put a time limit on the question, you can make it more difficult still.

But by decent questions I like the ones that at venue quizzes make teams discuss and think amongst themselves. Something a man does more than a woman remains my favourite of the Family Fortunes type. Endings of films are good for a video round.

Food and drink (5)

Due to age I can only instantly recall a handful of events over the years and the ones that stand out are largely due to great food and drink, or no food and drink. The university quiz for the eight people at 11am had no atmosphere; the betting quiz in central London after a 3 course gourmet meal with wine was spectacular.

For venue quizzes though you need to spend as much of your budget as possible on providing drink for the guests. Several of my clients use raffle tickets as drinks vouchers, which leads to an intriguing short-term black market in tokens during the quiz as the non-drinkers take bribes for the golden tickets. If you have spent a lot on the drinks, you can perhaps get away with a lower budget for the food. People will remember a good night if they've had a few drinks and will forget the tired sandwiches. If they have had nothing to drink, the sangers will stand out a mile.

I have been incredibly lucky to work with clients who have people who have really gone the extra mile when organising quiz nights. Several have decorated their offices, made name plates for the teams, furnished every table with all manner of crisps and sweets, provided a table plan so everyone can see where they are sat, and of course, laid on free food and drink.

At virtual quizzes people obviously sort themselves out. I have seen people necking Desperado, couples sink a bottle of red wine in the time it takes us to complete two rounds, and others just enjoying a nice cup of tea. The online events have also taken place as people have been eating their supper, cooking pizza, or doing the washing up. The advantage of all these activities when done remotely is they are not disruptive to any other guests in the slightest, thanks to the beauty of the Mute All feature.

Keep it flowing (6)

My early quiz events did use to overrun. At the London ones I remember clearly, as the time ticked past 9.30pm, a few getting their coats during the music round and heading to beat the rush for the Tube. After the first few events we made sure in the pre-quiz arrangements to agree a start time and run time with the organiser. This also avoided awkward situations if guests arrived late. There was some flexibility but for a quiz starting at 6.30 with a chef poised for 7.30 nosh, we started on the b of the bong.

With virtual quizzes, weight of numbers was the best way of starting on time. If I had 300 guests online, I was not going to wait for 10 or 20 latecomers, particularly given their broadband could disconnect any minute. A few of our Zoom events were a little more flexible with starting, when only 7 guests had registered, and at the start time it was just me and the organiser online.

The biggest complaint I saw when going to other quizzes was slow marking, or slow pace of the quiz in general. So for my events I always try to keep it moving. Venue quizzes I would ask the question twice, and then move on. If you are dealing with a group of very mixed ages, you may then need to repeat a question to a more mature team, but that could often be done off-mike.

Keep it competitive (7)

At venue quizzes, I read out the scores at the end of each round, and they were often displayed on screen. For virtual quizzes, the scoreboard is updated after each question. For regular clients I have a record of previous results, so can spot if a current leader, or team in contention, has won the quiz before. Conversely if a previous winner is having an absolute shocker, it provides material for banter with the crowd.

Team names help the spirit of competition and provide talking points for the host. You have probably noticed the chapter titles in this book which have all been used at ask-Tony events. My venue quizzes only ever used to feature a team competition. There was often dispute about the numbers on a team. Sometimes the venue or organiser was charging per individual and so encouraged large teams. Others, where people were placed into teams randomly, lent themselves to being equal numbers. Where there were a few issues was in the case of no-shows, for example a team called Quiz Team Aguilera who were scheduled to be six-person, unexpectedly being reduced to just two.

For virtual quizzes it was much easier to run an individual and a team element. Initially I did this by asking people to pre-register their team name, but it proved too complex to then match the individual, and their team name, to their Kahoot username. So in Kahoot I asked people to enter the team they were playing for during the quiz.

This did mean that for virtual quizzes people were predominantly playing as individuals. The banter and discussion on an answer between team mates as would take place in a venue was not present. As I previously mentioned, this did lead to individuals connecting during the quiz via WhatsApp or Facetime, but given they were all answering individually, you just tended to get a group of individuals in the same team either get the answer correct, or all get it wrong.

Self-policing (8)

If you are hosting a quiz for 100+ people at a venue, you cannot personally check everybody to see whether anybody is cheating. But you can lay out at the start the ground rules, and then leave it up to the audience to grass up anyone cheating. When newspapers were more of a thing, at London events during the first round I used between questions to confiscate copies of the Evening Standard. As a joke I once tried taking people's phones, but it was more hassle than it was worth. The suspected guilty party would usually insist they were checking on their babysitter or had an ill relative.

In team quizzes I have not found cheating to be a big problem as it is pretty obvious when it is going on, and other teams are not shy at pointing it out, and naming and shaming. For virtual events, whether a household has got a network of accomplices supplying the answers, or a bank of screens, has only really been an issue for the weekly events. You can reduce the time per question, or in extreme cases, just boot them out of the video call.

Banter (9)

At venues, I like to move around between questions and talk to the audience. At the start this will involve finding the team who were previous champions, or anybody celebrating a birthday. For the news round answers we will go round the tables and select somebody to answer a question on microphone. As the quiz progresses, I can highlight the contenders and those languishing near the bottom and respond to any lively characters that emerge. As the drink flows and we get into the music round, a few people start to get up and dance, and a few will grab the mike and belt out some karaoke. When prize time comes, the winners will pose for photos, and the losers will cry into their wooden spoons.

Virtually trying to recreate all that is much more difficult, as you can only really speak directly to one house at a time, and there is little outward audience feedback. You can potentially use the chat window to read out comments, a technique often used by talk radio stations, but that is still very much one-way.

Experiment and get feedback (10)

The biggest lesson I have taken from the twenty years running quiz nights has come in the last few months due to the instant feedback I get from every guest at any virtual event.

Looking back I should have included feedback forms from the venue quizzes, but chances are very few of the guests would have filled them in either physically or online. I never spent any time analysing the answer papers each team submitted, as they were often chucked out at the venue to avoid me taking 2,000 sheets of often beer-stained a4 home with me. I knew if a round had been particularly low-scoring and therefore too hard, but I didn't have the time or inclination to look for any other patterns that would have helped me write better quizzes.

The good news is that with virtual quizzes there is no shortage of data from each quiz and it is instantly available. Perhaps the most useful responses from guests is the suggested topics for next time. If the leading players get less than 70% answer accuracy, I know the questions are too hard. I can also look at average response time per topic and rounds that proved very popular.

The innovations in lockdown around the musical finish featuring the pets came from talking to the audience during the quiz. And we were able to try out new ideas the next week based on suggestions collected the previous week. I've also received dozens of potential questions from people who have enjoyed the quiz and wanted one of their favourites to be included in a round the following week.

There are other formats for doing virtual quizzes and it may be worth exploring those. You can just broadcast a set of questions to the world and leave people to answer, and mark, themselves. You can recreate the whole team quiz dynamic by using breakout rooms and introduce more creative rounds such as drawing by making more use of the annotate and screen-sharing tools.

But the thing I am looking forward to most? When it is safe to do so, being asked to come to a venue and host a physical quiz with some of the great characters and personalities I have met online over the past few months. It has been a great joy to see such a collection of friendly faces, of all ages, from all parts of the world.

Photo 23 A collage from one of the first virtual events in lockdown 2020

Photo 24 Some of the best looking pets from our musical finishes in 2020

Steve Roy is still hosting quiz nights.
You can book him via www.asktony.co.uk

Printed in Great Britain
by Amazon